From Baptist to Byzantium

How a Baptist Missionary
Traveled Halfway Around the
World
To Find the Ancient Orthodox
Faith

by

Father James Early

What if a former missionary penned a story about his journey to Orthodoxy in a writing style reminiscent of a good Southern Baptist? Suppose there was someone who could speak/write/teach like a Baptist though using newly discovered precepts of the ancient faith. That would be a rarity. Many adult converts to Orthodox Christianity leave behind not only their former beliefs, but also their former vocabulary. Then, especially if they write about it, they seem to acquire another tongue to tell the tale; or worse, their writing is laced with anger and resentment at their former denomination. Not here. Fr James Early writes like a Baptist who loves the Lord and as a seeker who traveled the world to, much to his surprise, find the Church.

The Rev. Fr. Joseph Huneycutt, assistant priest, St. George Orthodox Church, Houston, TX and author of *One Flew Over the Onion Dome* and *Defeating Sin*

Fr. James Early's book *From Baptist to Byzantium* is an absolute **must read** for all converts to the Orthodox Christian faith. His style is simple, clear and personable. Those who are lifelong "cradle" Orthodox will also be blessed and enlightened by it. The combination of his having been an engineer, a missionary, and a school teacher make him an excellent communicator of deep and important truths. Read it – you'll enjoy it! Having made a similar journey, being raised in a faithful Baptist family, going to a Baptist college, graduating from the same Baptist seminary as Fr. James, and having served 12 ½ years as a Baptist pastor and missionary, I fully entered into the struggles he describes so well in his book. Even if your denominational background is different than Fr. James' and mine, I believe you will be enlightened and encouraged by his and Jennifer's journey. If you are one who has struggled with your faith journey, this book will bless you.

The V. Rev. Fr. Gordon Walker, Pastor Emeritus, St. Ignatius Orthodox Church, Franklin, TN, and president, Grace Ministries, Inc.

In this moving story of his family's encounter with Eastern Orthodoxy, Father James Early reminds us that Truth often comes at a great price. But as he struggles to come to terms with ancient Orthodox Christianity – as he discovers Christ in the hearts of its people, in its doctrine, and in its worship – he also proves it is well worth the cost. This book is an excellent general introduction to the Orthodox faith, and a must-read for evangelical Christians involved with mission work in Orthodox countries.

Matthew Gallatin, Orthodox teacher, speaker, and author of *Thirsting for God in a Land of Shallow Wells* and the *Pilgrims from Paradise* podcast on Ancient Faith Radio

---

Remarkable things can happen to those who earnestly seek the Truth and courageously follow Christ wherever He leads them. Father James Early's account of discovering the richness of Orthodoxy through ministering to Bosnian Christians as a Baptist missionary will both inspire and enlighten its readers. What would possibly possess a family man to surrender a familiar environment, a secure income, and a solid reputation within his own faith community? I urge you to explore that question throughout the pages of this book and to find out for yourself how fulfilling and utterly persuasive the answer can be.

Molly Sabourin, author of the *Close to Home* weblog and Ancient Faith Radio podcast and contributing editor of *The Handmaiden* magazine.

God guides people to the Church in varied and often unexpected ways, and it is always a blessing to hear converts to Orthodoxy share their testimony – but Fr. James Early's account of how he went to Bosnia as a Baptist on a mission to convert the Serbs, and came back a convert to Orthodoxy, is one that is especially fascinating and edifying to read.

The Rev. Fr. John Whiteford, Pastor, St. Jonah of Manchuria Orthodox Church, Houston, TX, and author of *Sola Scriptura*

While on a mission to bring the Truth of Christ to the people of Bosnia, the author finds himself swept up into the heavenly worship of the indigenous Bosnian faithful. While honoring the strengths of his Baptist background, Fr. James recounts his own journey to the Holy Orthodox Church, plainly presenting how Orthodox Christianity shows itself to be not a replica of a first century faith community, but the Ancient Church itself. *From Baptist to Byzantium* will engage Evangelical seekers and resonate with Protestant missionaries who have served in Eastern European lands.

The Rev. Fr. Peter Jon Gillquist, Pastor, All Saints Orthodox Christian Church, Bloomington, IN, and best-selling recording artist

---

This book is an engaging account of the conversion to Orthodox Christianity by a Baptist missionary preacher, the personal and practical challenges he faced and his spiritual and intellectual struggle with theological questions raised when history and Scripture clashed with deeply-held, cherished beliefs. The unfolding of God's plan in the life of one young couple, their openness to following the path which the Holy Spirit gradually revealed to them and how their faith and trust in God sustained and guided them is both a unique personal story, but also one which will resonate with every reader.

Dr. Eugenia Constantinou, adjunct professor of biblical studies, University of San Diego, and host of the "Search the Scriptures" podcast on Ancient Faith Radio.

Acknowledgements

I would like to begin by thanking Fr. Peter Gillquist, Fr. Jordan Bajis, Fr. Paul O'Callaghan, Dr. Clark Carlton, and Kh. Frederica Mathewes-Green, who all took the time to write outstanding books designed to demonstrate the truth and beauty of Orthodoxy to non-Orthodox Christians. Had they not written their books, I might well not have found my way into the Ancient Faith. I know that I am just one of thousands of people who have discovered the joy of being Orthodox due to the labors of these writers.

I thank Fr. Gordon Walker for patiently answering my questions and for helping me decide to become Orthodox. Also, I appreciate his hosting me for a few days in 2002 and answering dozens more questions.

I appreciate all the encouragement that the readers of my weblog (http://saintjameskids.blogspot.com) gave me as I published a series of thirty entries that eventually became the core of this book. Their comments, questions, and suggestions gave me several good ideas for ways to expand the narrative.

I am grateful to Fr. Joseph Huneycutt and Fr. Matthew MacKay (my pastor) for reading through my manuscript and suggesting changes and additions. Also, Reader Michael and Jessica Fulton and my friend Clint Hale suggested many helpful changes, and they all worked very quickly.

I thank my children Audrey, Courtney, Beth and Christine, who many times had to hear me say "Daddy can't play tonight; I have to work on my book." Girls, I should have more time with you now!

Above all else, I am thankful for the countless hours that my beloved wife Jennifer spent reading, rereading, and suggesting excellent changes and additions. She is the best copy editor I could hope for. Without her loving encouragement and support, this project would not even be possible. If you like this book, please thank her as much as (perhaps even more than) you thank me!

From Baptist to Byzantium

ISBN – 978-1-928653-37-0
Regina Orthodox Press
Copyright © James Early 2009

Regina Orthodox Press
PO BOX 5288
Salisbury MA 01952
USA

800 636 2470

reginaorthodoxpress.com

TABLE OF CONTENTS

Father James Early

Preface

A strange phenomenon confronts almost all converts to Orthodoxy at one time or another. No matter how much time they spent in their former church or denomination, no matter how extensive their educational training in the collegiate and seminary system, no matter how deeply they are involved in its worship and teaching ministries, at some point the converts or the would-be converts go back to their "home church" and realize that they have become strangers in a strange land. More strange still is the fact that these one-time paragons of Reformation dogma and piety find themselves *more at home* in a temple filled with Byzantine frescoes (whether authentic or laminated), clouds of incense, and unmetered chanting than in the meeting houses of their youth. Such is the story of Fr. James and Khouria Jennifer Early.

If the climax to Fr. James' story is unremarkable, the journey there is most certainly worthy of note, for the Earlys were not merely devout Protestants; they were Southern Baptist *missionaries* to Bosnia! It is not unheard of, of course, for missionaries to go east looking to convert the Slavs and end up getting converted themselves. This has happened in Romania and Russia as well. But I feel a special kinship with the Earlys, since they were good "babdists," as I was once upon a time.

A few years ago Orthodox hackles were raised when a Southern Baptist missionary document entitled "Witnessing to Persons of Eastern Orthodox Background" started floating around the internet. Strangely enough, the Earlys' story confirms one of the major points of that document, namely that persons of

Orthodox background are difficult to convert! As Fr. James found, you can get Slavs to say the "sinner's prayer" and "give their hearts to Jesus," but it is extremely difficult to get them to leave the Orthodox Church for an Evangelical Church.

It was precisely this reticence to change churches that led Fr. James into a deeper study of the Orthodox Faith. And yet what strikes me about his story is not so much the intellectual struggles with this doctrine or that – we've all been there; done that – but the fact that he fell in love with Orthodox worship – even when he could not possibly have understood everything that was said. In reading his narrative it occurred to me that no one tried to convert him or his wife. There were no missionary calls on his house, no earnest young men trying to get him to renounce the *filioque* (did he even know what that was?). This confirms what I have been saying for quite a while now: the best way for the Orthodox Church to evangelize is simply to *be* Orthodox.

Jerusalem is the Mother of us all. Some Christian groups have traveled far indeed from Jerusalem, in spirit as well as in distance. Some have traveled so far that one strains in vain to detect any lingering resemblance to Mt Zion. Yet, even in the most deracinated and secular "churches" of today, that still, small voice echoes, however faintly: *Come home! Come home! Ye, who are weary, come home!* Fr James and Khouria Jennifer heard that call and answered it. *He who has ears to hear, let him hear.*

Clark Carlton
Repose of St Alexis Toth (2008)

Prologue

In the last forty years, a great number of Protestants and Roman Catholics around the world have chosen to leave their religious traditions and to unite themselves with the Orthodox Church. Many of these converts have written and published accounts of their pilgrimage to the Ancient Faith, so many so that Orthodox conversion stories have practically become a sub-genre of Orthodox literature. Most, if not all, of those who have published the story of their journey to Orthodoxy have writing skills that exceed my own. So why am I adding another such story to the burgeoning list?

Every Orthodox conversion story is unique and interesting. Although all of us converts have arrived at the same destination, we have traveled along very different paths, encountering and overcoming unique obstacles. After having related my own experience dozens of times, I have noticed a recurring reaction: Person after person has commented that my story is "amazing" or "fascinating" or "different," or something similar (some of my former missionary colleagues would say "insane," but more on that later...). After all, few evangelical missionaries who serve in Eastern Europe decide to convert to Orthodoxy. And to the best of my knowledge, none of those who have done so have yet published their conversion story. After about a dozen people urged me to put my story into writing, I finally decided that perhaps it was time for me to overcome my own laziness and just do it.

Before beginning the story, however, I must issue a disclaimer. In this book, I will not attempt to provide a great deal of argument for the correctness of Orthodox theological positions over and against those of the Roman

Catholic and Protestant traditions. Other books, most notably *Becoming Orthodox* by Fr. Peter Gillquist, *Common Ground* by Fr. Jordan Bajis, *Thirsting for God* by Matthew Gallatin, and especially Clark Carlton's four-part series on the Orthodox faith, do an excellent job at this endeavor. Nor will I always go into great detail about precisely *why* I found the Orthodox position on a particular issue compelling.

Rather, in writing this book, I desire to simply relate the story of how God led one ordinary man and his family through a series of adventures and radical changes, through eleven cities and three countries, to finally find a home in the One, Holy, Catholic and Apostolic Church. My prayer is that this story might edify and inspire those who read it, particularly non-Orthodox Christians who are curious about Orthodoxy. Above all else, my desire is that through this book, the Lord Jesus Christ might be glorified. Now unto Him be all glory, honor and praise, now and ever and unto the ages of ages!

From Baptist to Byzantium

Chapter One: Praeparatio Evangelio[1]

> *Before I formed you in the womb I knew you;*
> *Before you were born I sanctified you;*
> *I ordained you a prophet to the nations.*
> — JEREMIAH 1:5

Beginnings

The year 1967 was a time of great change for American society. Young people's hair was growing longer, while their patience with their parents was growing shorter. American involvement in the Vietnam War was increasing, as was opposition to the war. Racial hostility erupted in riots in Detroit and other major cities all around the nation. Tensions between the United States and the communist world remained high, with communist China exploding its first hydrogen bomb. The hippie movement was picking up steam, urged on by popular music groups like the Beatles, who assured that "All you need is love."

The year promised to also be momentous for a forty-seven-year-old Pentagon official named Cleland Early. After twenty-six years as an officer in the United States Marine Corps, including four years fighting in World War II and one year's service in Korea, Colonel Early was planning to retire. He was looking forward to working in the private sector, settling down somewhere with his family, and making his fortune. His forty-five-year-old wife Bettye had grown tired of the life of a military wife and was longing for stability. Having endured long periods of separation from Cleland during which she single-handedly raised their three children, she was ready to have a normal life. She longed to finally be able to travel

---

[1] Latin for "Preparation for the Gospel" I am indebted to Clark Carlton for this chapter title.

around the country, visiting places other than those where Cleland was assigned.

Cleland and Bettye's oldest daughter, Barbara, was about to graduate from college and begin life on her own. Their son Cleland Jr., age fourteen, and their younger daughter Lisa, eleven, would follow in the not-too-distant future. Their lives were happy and promised to get even better. And in ten short years, Cleland and Bettye would have the house all to themselves, with many years remaining to enjoy their lives together.

All of their plans changed, however, one day early in the summer of that tumultuous year. In June, Bettye began feeling ill and went to see the family doctor. The doctor's news proved to be a great shock to the whole family – Bettye was going to have another baby! She could not believe the doctor's words. How could she be pregnant at such an advanced age? Wouldn't the baby be at great risk for birth defects or other types of problems? At first, she found herself in a state of shock which soon changed to depression. She did not know what to do. Finally, however, she resolved to make the best of it, have the baby, and begin the process of parenting a small child all over again.

On March 8 of the following year, I made my entrance into the world. My early childhood was happy, and I was well cared for. My siblings adored me, doting on me and helping to take care of me.

Meanwhile, since my father's retirement from the Marine Corps, he had been working for a defense contractor in northern Virginia. He would go on to work in a total of three jobs in three different cities until 1974, when he accepted a position as a high school Marine ROTC instructor in Pasadena, Texas, a suburb of Houston. My mother, my sister Lisa, and I joined him there the following year, and so it was at the age of seven that I settled down in the city where I would grow up and where I would later work. Lisa went off to college the next year, and from then on my siblings were all in college or the work force. As a result, I spent most of my childhood living much like an only child, with parents who were the same age as most of my friends' grandparents. They loved me and took good care of me, but they were usually too busy or tired to spend much time with me.

My parents were decent, moral people who imparted to me a strong sense of right and wrong. Still, neither of them had much interest in God or the Bible, and we very rarely attended any type of church. My only memory of anything even remotely religious was attending an Episcopal school for the first half of my kindergarten year, where on at least one occasion I was spanked by the priest/principal for some type of misbehavior (probably talking too much!). From the time I was old enough to have an opinion about spiritual matters, I considered myself a staunch agnostic. I never gave much thought to whether or not I believed in God, and I certainly never read the Bible. I was at the very least a functional atheist. Little did I know that this would soon change dramatically!

Movement

Soon after I started high school, I began to awaken from my spiritual slumber. In the fall of my freshman year, I somehow managed to catch the eye of a sophomore girl. Unlike me, she was both attractive and popular, and I felt lucky just to have her. Her condition for us "going together" (remember that delightful term?) was that I go to church with her, at least occasionally. I figured that keeping her was well worth my enduring a few church services, so I agreed to her terms. I had no desire at all to set foot in a church of any denomination, and I expected to be thoroughly bored. Surprisingly, however, when I did attend services at her Church of Christ congregation, I was struck by the minister's challenging and practical sermons. For the first time in my life, I began to give some thought to God and the Bible.

About two months later, my female friend unceremoniously dumped me for an older, cooler, and more attractive guy. Along with our relationship, my church attendance came to an end. Before long, however, I experienced an ironic twist of what seemed at the time like fate. At the beginning of the next school year, I found myself "going with" my former girlfriend's younger sister (no laughing!), and as you might expect, I found myself back in the same pew in the same church, once again being challenged by the same minister's sermons. Unfortunately, this relationship was to be almost as short-lived as the previous one, and before long, I was once again not even, to use St. James's phrase, a "hearer of the Word."

Nevertheless, my second stint in the sisters' church did lead to a major turning point in my life, for it was then that I was inspired to start reading the Bible and going to church on my own, and not just because some girl said I had to. I asked my mother if we could start going to church, and she gladly agreed. Since she was from an Episcopal background, we began attending a local Episcopal parish where she was a member. This parish became my church home for the rest of my high school years.

I was fortunate that my new church home was not a liberal or heretical parish. Our rector was a pious man who ascribed to traditional Christianity and who clearly loved the Lord and his flock. He occasionally went on mission trips and even learned Spanish (while in his fifties!) so that he could start an outreach to the many Hispanic families that lived around the church. Still, his sermons were more like literary analyses than true biblical preaching, and they lacked the application to life that I had heard in the preaching in my friends' churches. In addition, the liturgy seemed dry and uninspiring to me, and very few of the kids in the youth group seemed to be serious about their Christian faith. One of them once asked me, "Why do you go to church?" I said, "Because I love God!" (Sadly, this was not quite true, but it seemed like a good answer at the time!) He quite seriously replied, "I never thought of that. I wish that were my reason!"

All of these experiences led me to think that there had to be something more out there. I now believed in God, and I felt like I needed to worship and get to know Him. I wanted to be involved in church, but I also longed for stronger, life-based preaching and teaching and a more meaningful worship experience. Enter the Baptists…

Receiving Jesus

In addition to the girls who introduced me to the Church of Christ, I was blessed to make several other Christian friends during my high school years. All four of my closest friends happened to be Southern Baptists, members of the largest Protestant denomination in the United States. Each of these friends frequently invited me to attend services and youth outreach events at their churches, and occasionally, they prevailed upon me to go with them. I was particularly interested in the events at which meals were served. I specifically remember one time when a friend asked me to go to a youth meeting, and I asked, "Will there be food?" When he replied in the affirmative, I said "Absolutely!" (Note to all youth leaders: Never underestimate the power of pizza!)

Nearly every time I went to a church service or youth event, I heard preaching that was powerful, biblical, and relevant to my life. Speaker after speaker challenged me to quit living for myself and to fully devote myself to God. Many of them challenged me and the rest of the audience to do something I had never heard of – "get saved." They told me that if I would simply accept Jesus as my personal Lord and Savior, that all my sins would be forgiven and that I would be guaranteed entrance to heaven after I died. This sounded pretty good to me, and I cannot tell you how many times I raised my hand (usually "with every head bowed and every eye closed") or signed a card saying that I was giving my life to Jesus. Still, these "decisions" never stuck, and I would soon return to my old self-centered lifestyle. I was very interested in going to heaven and receiving God's blessing for this life, but I was unwilling to make any changes to my life in order to do so. As a result, God, the church, and the Bible remained little more than a hobby for me.

In addition to bringing me to church events, my friends also frequently testified to me about their personal faith in God and in Jesus Christ. Slowly but surely, bit by bit, they broke through my stubbornness and skepticism and convinced me of many of the fundamental truths that I still hold today, including God's love for us, the truthfulness of the Scriptures, and the importance of regular Bible study and worship. Although I often rejected what they had to say, they never gave up on me; instead, they patiently and lovingly shared their beliefs with me in a way that was never judgmental or condemning. And while nearly all the speakers that I heard at the services were helpful, the personal witness of my friends was invaluable.

By the time I moved to Austin to attend college, I decided it was time to explore some other Christian traditions besides the Episcopal Church. During my first semester, I lived on campus and had no car. This led me to visit nearly every church that was within walking distance: Baptist, Methodist, non-denominational, and yes, even Episcopal. Nearly every Sunday, I visited services at a different type of church. None of the churches I visited during this semester made much of an impression on me. Sadly, at this time, I had not even heard of the Orthodox Church, even though I lived within walking distance from St. Elias' Orthodox Church, near downtown Austin.

In January, I moved off campus, into an apartment that was a few blocks away from a very large Southern Baptist church. Naturally, I decided to give the church a try. The strong preaching there reminded me of what I had heard at my high school friends' churches, and the seriousness with which the people there seemed to take their faith greatly impressed me. The short distance from my apartment didn't hurt either!

Although I still felt some loyalty to the Episcopal Church, primarily due to my love for my mother, by the end of my freshman year I felt like I could no longer remain in that tradition. The Baptist church's preaching, along with the enthusiasm of its people, was something that I had never seen in my own church, and it drew me like a magnet. I correctly guessed that my mother would be hurt by my decision, but I prayed that she would agree to disagree with me about religion.

She eventually did, although my decision to leave the Episcopal Church caused tension between us for several years.

For the next two years, I alternated between living in Austin and living in my parents' home in Pasadena, where I worked as an engineering co-op student at IBM in Clear Lake City, south of Houston. In my church involvement, I alternated between my church in Austin and various Baptist and other evangelical churches near my parents' house. In spite of attending church fairly regularly and staying in touch with my high school friends, I still remained unwilling to change my life or fully dedicate my life to Christ. I wanted the ruler of my life to be *me*, not God.

During those two years, however, I became convinced that I could not be my own ruler and receive all the blessings of Christianity at the same time. I also began to understand that just making a profession of faith in Christ was not enough. I had made dozens of such professions, but these types of "decisions" had demonstrated no power to transform. What I needed was to not only believe, but to resolve to live as Christ commanded me to live. After years of resisting God, I finally gave in. On January 15, 1989, at the end of the morning worship service at my church in Austin, when the invitation was given, I went forward and once and for all dedicated my life to Christ. I was baptized a week later, and I thus became a full-fledged member of the Christian tradition to which I thought I would belong for the rest of my life.

Chapter Two: Growth

Therefore, my beloved, as you have always obeyed, not as in my presence only, but now much more in my absence, work out your own salvation with fear and trembling; for it is God who works in you both to will and to do for His good pleasure.
— PHILIPPIANS 2:12-13

Involvement

Before I had made my profession of faith, I had been more interested in *appearing* to be a godly person than in actually *becoming* one. By the time I joined the Baptist church, however, I truly desired to grow spiritually. Accordingly, I jumped into the activities of my newly adopted church with enthusiasm. I immediately started attending Sunday School, worship on Sunday morning and evening, and a college Bible study on Friday evenings; I even joined the college choir. Still, I desperately needed a spiritual mentor, but I was too young and spiritually immature to know to look for one. As a result, my spiritual growth was minimal, despite all my church activity. Before long, I had fallen back into some of my old bad habits and found myself living a life that was not radically different from the one that I had led before my conversion. My life showed little or no evidence of the change that the Gospel can bring.

One of the church activities in which I became involved was a weekly Friday night Bible study series that was held in one of several church members' homes. This study would draw anywhere between 50-100 college students each week. Best of all, the host fed us each week! At about the third study I attended, I found myself at a table with three girls. The one across from me was a preacher's daughter from northeast Texas. She was a diminutive, soft-spoken and very attractive blonde named Jennifer. Jennifer and I quickly became friends, even though I soon began dating another girl.

After a couple of months, however, this dating relationship fell apart, and I decided to call Jennifer and ask her if she would like to go out with me. To my delight, she agreed! Soon, we began to date regularly, and by the end of 1989, we had begun to discuss marriage. We had much in common, including a love for the Bible and the church and a desire to serve God with our lives. The following September, we were married.

Georgetown

Three months later, I graduated from college and accepted a position as an electrical engineer with International Paper in Georgetown, South Carolina. I was not at all excited about the prospect of working in a paper mill, much less one halfway across the country. Still, the paper mill job was the best offer that I had, and Jennifer and I felt that we had no other choice. Little did I know that God would use our experience in South Carolina to lead us down an exciting path that we could not have envisioned.

In the small town in South Carolina where we lived, there was little to do other than go to church. So, we did – every time it was open. Freed from the distractions of college life, I finally began to grow spiritually. For the first time in my life, I began to seriously study the Scriptures and to try to apply their teachings to my life. I began to be involved in both evangelistic and humanitarian outreach projects. I was asked to teach high school Sunday School, and Jennifer and I led a weeknight Bible study for youth. Most importantly, I began to understand what it meant to orient all facets of my life toward God.

At the same time, however, I became increasingly dissatisfied with my job. I had gradually lost all interest in engineering during college and had more than once seriously considered changing my major to history. My father repeatedly persuaded me to stay with engineering, however. I had attended college on a full scholarship, but about 75% of the scholarship was tied to studying engineering. My father informed me that if I dropped engineering, I would have to make up the lost scholarship money on my own. Upon hearing this, I had decided that perhaps I could stick it out just a little longer! Plus, I kept hearing from professors and fellow students that working in the "real world" would be much more enjoyable than school. So, I had decided to give the engineering profession a try.

Unfortunately, I found that working in the "real world" (or at least in my job) was no more enjoyable than school had been. After about nine months on the job, I decided to pursue my love of history by applying to some masters' degree programs. I soon had my future all mapped out. Jennifer and I and our new baby daughter Audrey would return to Texas, I would earn a masters and a PhD in history, and then I would get a job somewhere as a history professor.

When I spoke to my pastor about my plans, he suggested that I consider working toward becoming a Church History professor in a Baptist seminary. I thought, "Why not? It's worth a look!" and I sent off for a catalog from Southwestern Baptist Theological Seminary in Fort Worth, Texas. After receiving the catalog, I read through it and soon realized that to become a professor in seminary, I would first have to take a large number of courses that I had little interest in, such as Greek, Hebrew, and theology. I just wanted to study history! So, I filed the catalog away on the shelf, thinking I would never look at it again. But God had other plans for me.

Calling

One day in December of 1991 I was not feeling well, and so I stayed home from work. That afternoon, while sitting at my desk, my attention was suddenly and unexpectedly directed toward the seminary catalog that was still on my shelf. In an instant, I somehow knew that God wanted me to go to that seminary and study toward a career in full-time Christian ministry. My desire to begin a masters program in history (along with about $100 in application fees) was instantly gone. Although I heard no audible voice, I believed (and still believe) that this was God speaking to me, through my heart and my mind.

To my great relief, when I revealed my call experience to Jennifer, she was very supportive, saying "I'm not at all surprised." She was completely open to being the wife of a full-time minister. So, Jennifer and I began planning to return to our home state and for me to begin seminary. With my pastor's encouragement, I started teaching adult classes and preaching in our church and other churches in their pastor's absence. I redoubled my personal Bible study discipline and developed a love for theology and biblical languages. Jennifer and I were both excited about returning to Texas and being near our families again. That is, we were until the reality of what we were about to do hit home.

Reality

For a month or so after Jennifer and I decided to respond to God's call to attend seminary, I was filled with enthusiasm. I was excited to have a reason to escape the paper mill and start doing something I had at first not cared for, but which I had since grown to love—studying Christian history and theology. I announced our decision before our whole congregation, and everyone there, especially our pastor, treated us like heroes.

But then I started looking at the financial ram-ifications of our decision. As an engineer, I was earning a comfortable living, so much so that Jennifer was able to stay home with our baby daughter Audrey. But we realized that quitting my job would mean that we would both have to take near-minimum wage jobs, because even though I had an engineering degree, I had learned almost no real engineering skills. Worse still, since I would only be able to work part time, Jennifer would have to work full time, and Audrey would have to go into day care.

Like a good mathematician, I started crunching numbers, estimating our expenses and our likely meager earnings. Fortunately, the seminary owned some apartments, and they rented them at a very low cost. I ordered a scale drawing of the floor plan of an apartment, and I actually drew the model on some graph paper, trying to see where we would fit our few worldly possessions. I remember saying to Jennifer, "There's not even room for a desk chair in this tiny place! I will have to sit on the bed when I study!" It quickly became clear to us that we would have to sell about half of our furniture just to fit into the apartment.

Soon I realized that even with the low cost of living in a 700-square foot apartment, we would not be able to earn near enough to make ends meet. One evening, in tears, I said to Jennifer, "We can't do this. There is just no way!" Thankfully, I married a woman of great faith, very often greater than my own. She said to me, "James, if God is calling us to go to seminary, don't you think that He will provide for our needs?" I had to admit that she was right. So, the following fall, we loaded up a small moving van and headed for Fort Worth.

Chapter Three: Seminary

I heard the voice of the Lord, saying:
"Whom shall I send,
And who will go for Us?"
Then I said, "Here am I! Send me."
— ISAIAH 6:8

Provision

My seminary years were a very difficult time for us. Not only did Jennifer have to work full-time, with Audrey going into day care, but I also had little time to spend with my family. The first year was especially challenging. I attended classes all morning, worked all afternoon painting seminary-owned houses and apartments, and studied all evening. During my first semester, I also served as the interim music director at a small country church forty-five minutes from Fort Worth. Since the church had services Sunday morning and evening, we had to spend the whole day there each Sunday. My service at the church ended in January, when the church hired a permanent music director. This left us very short on funds, and I had to take on all the extra work I could. I spent nearly every weekend doing odd jobs: painting houses, cutting grass, doing custodial work, helping people move, and filling in for absent preachers and music directors.

These were lean times, but God brought us through it all. One time when Jennifer and I were driving home from church, we were discussing how we were going to put food on the table the next day, because our checking account was empty. When we looked at our back door, we saw an envelope taped to the door with twenty dollars inside. Typed on the envelope was Philippians 4:19: "My God shall supply all of your needs according to His riches in glory in Christ Jesus." This was exactly what we needed to make it to our next paycheck! And this was not a one-time occurrence: mysterious checks and cash seemed to arrive with regular irregularity.

In the summer between my first and second years of seminary, I heard about a new Christian school that was about to open in a nearby town. I thought, "Well, I have no teaching credentials or experience, but I know an awful lot of math and science, so why not? I'll apply." I didn't think I had any chance of getting hired. But after I talked to the headmaster for about half an hour, he hired me on the spot. This meant a big pay increase, meaning less work for me on weekends and more time to spend with Jennifer and Audrey. Plus, the school's unique schedule enabled me to teach only three days a week, so that I could take a full load of classes on the other two days. Each year, I was given an additional class to teach, resulting in still greater pay. Jennifer was even able to cut back to working part time after my first year of teaching. And, although I did not know it at the time, my experience with teaching math and science would pay off greatly in the future.

Other than the financial strain, seminary was a great time of learning for us all. I was able to immerse myself in my two new favorite subjects of theology and Church History. I also enjoyed studying Hebrew, Greek and other disciplines related to Christian ministry. Jennifer and I both participated in several in-depth Bible and theological studies through our local church. Most significantly, for the first time I learned the importance of a daily time of prayer and meditation on the Scriptures, habits that have stayed with me to this day. My intensive study of the Scriptures also had a side effect that I had not anticipated: it raised many questions about the meaning of certain passages, questions that my professors and pastors could never answer to my satisfaction. Little did I know it, but these questions would not be answered until many years later when I discovered Orthodoxy.

As is true in many, if not most, evangelical seminaries, my Church History professor spent very little time on Orthodoxy. My first encounter with Orthodox theology occurred in the fall of 1993, when I took a course entitled "Missions in Eastern Europe." The professor, a Romanian Baptist leader, had us watch a film on the basics of Orthodoxy. I remember writing a paper on the film, in which I stated that some of the teachings of Orthodoxy seemed sound, but others, including the Church's doctrine of salvation, were clearly unacceptable in my opinion. The professor also required us to read *The Orthodox Church* by Bishop Kallistos Ware. I had no interest in reading this book, so I whipped through the whole thing in a weekend. As you can guess, I did not get much out of my reading. This would be the only Orthodox book I would read until seven years later, when I again picked up the same book and read it – with a very different result.

Marching Orders

When I first sensed a calling toward vocational Christian ministry, I did not know what specific area of service I was to pursue. I simply sensed that God wanted me to go to seminary, study, and wait for further instruction. At first I just assumed that I would pastor a church, which was the goal of the overwhelming number of students at the seminary. After my interim music position ended, I began applying to area churches that were in need of a pastor. After several months of not receiving any replies, one church finally contacted me. I preached before this church once and was even invited back for a second "tryout," but in the end they chose someone else. This lack of success in landing a pastorate led me to believe that perhaps God did not want me to be a pastor at that time. Perhaps He had something else in mind for me.

One thing that I had no interest in doing was serving as a foreign missionary. During the spring of my first year in seminary, the seminary held its annual Missions Conference, which was primarily a tool used by our denominational missions society for recruiting potential missionaries. There was a lot of hype and excitement about the conference. I decided to completely avoid it, so that I would not get caught up in a cloud of emotion, walk down the aisle, and sign myself and my family up for missions. After the conference was over, I thought to myself, "Whew! I dodged that bullet!"

But the "bullet" turned out to be more like a boomerang. It came back to hit me one day in the most unlikely of circumstances. One day I was sitting and reading a required textbook on Baptist history. I was reading a section about Baptist beginnings in Eastern Europe in the mid-nineteenth century. As I read about Western European Baptist missionaries spreading their faith in places such as Hungary, Romania, and Russia, I sensed that God was telling me, "This is what you are going to do." Of course, God did not reveal to me that I was going to go there to eventually become Orthodox – if He had, I probably wouldn't have gone. Instead, He gave me just as much as I could handle at the time.

Jennifer and I both struggled with this new calling. We understood that a career in foreign missions would mean rarely seeing family and friends. We would have to learn a new language and culture, and we would have to give up our comfortable suburban life. Jennifer in particular worried about Audrey growing without the benefit of regular contact with her extended family. One day, however, Jennifer was reading through the part of the Sermon on the Mount where Jesus asks, "What man is there among you who, if his son asks for bread, will give him a stone? Or if he asks for a fish, will he give him a serpent? If you then, being evil, know how to give good gifts to your children, how much more will your Father who is in heaven give good things to those that ask Him?" (Matt. 7:9-11). After this, Jennifer realized that God's love for Audrey was much greater than hers, and that His call for our lives was also a call on Audrey's life, and that He would provide for her needs.

After this, Jennifer and I both felt complete peace about answering the call to missions. We spent the remaining two years of seminary preparing for a career as missionaries. We took an in-depth evangelism training course during my second year of seminary, and I became the director of the training program my third year. During my fourth year, we helped start a new church in south Fort Worth. As we looked ahead to life after school, we felt certain that we were supposed to go to Eastern Europe, but we had no idea to which country. So, I decided to "scope out" a country through a short-term mission trip.

Chapter Four: Missions

> *...praying also for us, that God would open to us a door for the word, to speak the mystery of Christ...that I may make it manifest, as I ought to speak.*
>
> — COLOSSIANS 4:3-4

Prague

For about two years after I received my calling into international mission service, I had kept my eyes open for a short-term trip that I could join, so that I might gain a small taste of what missionary service would be like. Opportunities were abundant, but none of those I learned about seemed right until early 1995, when I met a local pastor who had been taking a group of people to the Czech Republic each year since the fall of communism. He was planning to take another group in May of that year, and he was looking for more people to go with the group. I prayed about this and talked to Jennifer, and soon I was convinced that going on the trip was the right thing to do. However, funding was a problem, since the trip was going to cost about $1600, and we had nowhere near that much money to spare. Thankfully, the missions committee at the church where Jennifer and I attended agreed to fund the trip in full – yet another answered prayer!

While in the Czech Republic, my group and I traveled around with a local Czech Baptist pastor, speaking about our faith in local churches, retirement homes, and even in several public school classrooms (can you imagine that?). Most of the people to whom we spoke were young and had lived their entire lives under a communist regime that had persecuted all religious traditions. Many people in our audience were very interested in what we had to say. The spiritual interest of the young people to whom we spoke greatly impacted me, as did the warm hospitality and friendliness of the Czech people.

During the trip, I met a Southern Baptist missionary who was the pastor of the English-language International Baptist Church in Prague, the capital city. As I told him about my desire to serve as a missionary in Eastern Europe, he became excited. He said, "I have been looking for someone to come here and help me try to reach the large international student population for quite some time. Would you like to come help me?" I told him I would think and pray about it, and that I still had a year of seminary to go. After thinking, praying, and discussing it for a couple of months, Jennifer and I decided that we would accept the missionary's offer. When we called the missionary in Prague and told him, he was thrilled. He immediately wrote a job request for us and sent it to the central office of the International Mission Board, the mission organization supported by churches that are a part of the Southern Baptist Convention.

A year later, I graduated from seminary, and about six weeks after that, we were on a plane to Prague. Unfortunately for us, the missionary who invited us to Prague decided to resign due to health problems and to return to the States. He and his family were in Prague for only ten days after our arrival, barely enough time to get us oriented. Then, about two weeks after our sponsors left, another missionary family came to take their place. They were veteran missionaries who had already served in two other countries, one for over ten years. They were a great help to us, but of course, they had no more knowledge of Prague or its international student population than we did. So, instead of having someone tell us what to do and how to do it, we were going to have to figure out how to do our assignment from scratch.

Initially, our time in Prague was very difficult for all of us. Not only did we have to learn a new language and culture, but we had to adjust to a lifestyle very different from what we had been used to in Texas. We had no car, and so we had to walk or take public transport (which fortunately is excellent in Prague) everywhere we went. We had to go to the grocery store every day, buying only what we could carry home. We lived in a small, one bedroom apartment. Audrey, who was five at the time, did not even have her own room—she had to sleep on a sleeper sofa in the living room! We had no phone line for the first month or so, and after we did get one, it only worked about half the time.

In addition to all this, we struggled with the climate. The summers were nice and mild, but the winters were brutal, especially for us Texans. During the winter, the temperature routinely dropped below zero degrees; one morning, it reached minus 23 degrees Celsius. We had double windows, with a space in between. We kept our milk in this space, so as to save space in our tiny refrigerator. One morning, we pulled the milk out only to find that it was frozen, despite the fact that it was technically inside our apartment! Also, the amount of daylight in the winter was depressingly small. At the peak of winter, the sun rose at about 8:30 and set at about 3:30. Needless to say, we had never experienced life like this before, and we thought that our lives were really tough. Eventually, however, we realized that our lives were not as difficult as we had first thought. We had lived a very comfortable, almost pampered, suburban life in the U.S., and now we were simply getting a taste of the urban life that much of the rest of the world lived. Before long, we had become more or less used to our new lifestyle.

The greatest challenge that I faced was not having any clue at all how to do my job. I had gone from being a highly competent teacher and church worker to a person who was far less than competent. Although I did undertake a few productive ministry tasks – teaching Sunday School, helping lead worship and preaching occasionally at our church, and leading a home Bible study for adults, I was bothered by the fact that I was not really doing what I had been brought to Prague to do. After several months of research and talking with other ministry groups in Prague, I finally did find a dormitory full of international students, and I began planning outreach events for them. After conducting a couple of fellowship and outreach events with the students in the dorm, I felt that my student ministry was finally rolling. Little did I know, however, that it was about to make a dramatic turn and begin rolling in an entirely different direction.

Change of Scenery

In 1991, the Federal Republic of Yugoslavia began to break apart. The following year, the former Yugoslav republic of Bosnia broke out into a disastrous civil war in which nearly 100,000 people were killed and nearly two million were displaced over a four year period. The war formally ended in November of 1995 with the signing of the Dayton Accord. At that time, the Bosnian state was divided into two autonomous entities: the Muslim/Croat Federation and the Serb Republic. Scattered throughout Bosnia, particularly in the Federation, were a small number of national Baptists and other evangelical Christians. Their leaders, with the help of the Croatian Baptist Union, had conducted humanitarian work throughout Bosnia during the war and had won a substantial number of converts. When the war ended, these leaders appealed to our mission agency to send some missionaries to help expand their work.

Needless to say, there were not a large number of Western missionaries flocking to serve in war-torn Bosnia, which was peaceful only because of the 60,000 or so NATO troops stationed there. Eventually, however, four veteran missionary couples who were near retirement agreed to serve for six months until longer-term volunteers could be found. They began arriving in September of 1996. Part of their task was continuing the humanitarian work that had begun during the war by various Baptist organizations. But their main job was to work with groups of converts to the Baptist faith, leading Bible studies that would ultimately lead to churches. Two of the couples went to the northeastern town of Tuzla, which had not been damaged nearly as much as other parts of the country, including Sarajevo.

Meanwhile, one day in January of 1997, while Jennifer and I were reading our mission agency's monthly magazine, we came across an urgent appeal for more volunteers to go to Bosnia. The initial volunteers' terms were almost up, and still no one had stepped forth to replace them. As I read the appeal, it happened again: The Lord seemed to speak to me in that mysterious, voiceless manner that I had experienced twice before. He seemed to be telling me: "*You* will be one of their replacements!" I spoke to Jennifer about it, and she agreed to consider the possibility of relocating to Bosnia. We knew that it would be a big adjustment to transplant our lives once again, this time to a war-torn nation. But once again, we remembered that if God were calling us to make this move, He would give us the strength to do His work, even in this difficult place.

The next thing we had to do was to obtain permission to make this big move. We were serving a two-year term, and the policy of the mission board was that two-year volunteers do not move in the middle of their terms. Around the first of February, I shared our desire with our supervisor and asked him, "Is it even possible for us to do this?" After speaking to his supervisor, he said, "It's not only possible, we want and need you to go!" We were given a month to get ready and say our goodbyes. Then, on March 7, a missionary in Croatia arrived in the van that would carry us and our things to our new home. One of the first things he said to us was, "Well, are you ready to go to Bosnia?"

Crossing

The trip to Bosnia took two days. The first thirty hours or so were uneventful. But soon after we crossed the Croatian border the van's battery light came on. We decided that we had best not stop, lest the car not start again. Unfortunately, however, Audrey became carsick, and we finally had to stop at a roadside gas station. Sure enough, the van would not start again. While we were trying to figure out what to do, a group of men walked up to the van. They seemed to want to help, but none of them knew any English.

At that time, I only spoke about twenty words of Serbo-Croatian, but this was twenty words more than anyone else in our group knew. As a result, I was quickly elected spokesman of our traveling band. Not surprisingly, I had no idea what the men were saying, nor could I explain our situation to them. One of the men finally used hand signals to indicate that we should open the hood. We did so, and he examined the engine compartment. He looked at me and said "Mo-tor! Ka-POOT!" This I understood clearly! Fortunately, it was the battery, not the motor that was "ka-poot," but in any case, we appeared to be stuck. There was no way to get a new battery, because it was late Saturday night, we were in the middle of nowhere, and everything was closed (there were no 24-hour Wal-Marts in Croatia!).

Finally, the men decided to give us a push-start. This worked nicely, and we were soon on our way again. As long as we didn't stop again, we would be in great shape! Unfortunately, another stop was inevitable. To enter Bosnia, we had to cross a river, and all the bridges across the river had been destroyed during the war. We would have to take a ferry, and we had heard that sometimes one had to wait in line for an hour or more just to get to the ferry.

After two more tense hours of driving, we finally made it to the line for the ferry. The van died about three times while we were waiting, but fortunately, we were able to push-start it each time. Finally, we drove onto the ferry. You can guess what happened next: the van died. It took about twenty minutes for the ferry to cross the river. Our plan was to push-start it yet again right before we reached the Bosnian side. This plan was complicated by two factors: first, the ferry was jam-packed with cars, and second, the road leading away from the makeshift dock went up a steep incline.

Once we were across the river, we were unable to push-start the van. I tried to see if we could get some help from the ferry operators, but they had no interest in helping us. Instead, they just loaded up the ferry from the Bosnian side, and we had to ride backwards across the river to Croatia again. We were starting to wonder if we would ever get off the ferry!

After we arrived back on the Croatian side and the cars headed for Croatia were all off, I noticed that the first car in line was a white Jeep Cherokee with "UN" marked on the side. I thought, "If the driver works for the UN, then he probably speaks English, and maybe he will help us!" As he drove onto the ferry, I frantically waved my arms and tried to signal him to pull in right in front of us. He complied and then got out of his car.

In perfect English, he asked me, "So, where are you going?" "Tuzla," I replied. "Really?!?" he replied, "That is where I live! So, what will you be doing there?" "Missionary work," I replied somewhat cautiously. "Wonderful!" he exclaimed. "I am the pastor of the evangelical church in Tuzla." So not only was he employed by the United Nations, but he was also a fellow evangelical believer and minister of the Gospel! As we continued talking, he produced a piece of rope and used it to tie our van to his jeep. Then, when we reached the other side, this Good Samaritan towed us into Bosnia. Jennifer and I believed then, and still believe today, that God must have sent this man to help us. If not, it was an awfully strange coincidence!

After we reached the other side, he offered to tow us all the way to Tuzla, a trip of about 50 miles, but which would take an hour and a half due to the various NATO checkpoints along the away. We called our colleague in Tuzla who was waiting on us, and he immediately set out to come meet us with an extra battery and escort us back to Tuzla. We thanked our rescuer profusely and told him goodbye. When our colleague arrived, we slowly and carefully followed him the rest of the way to Tuzla. Our trip was made all the more perilous by the fact that we did not use our headlights for fear of running down our new battery. At about midnight, we finally arrived in Tuzla. It was my twenty-ninth birthday. Our adventure was over. Or, to be more accurate, it was just beginning...

Life in Tuzla

At about five o'clock our first morning in Tuzla, we awoke to hear a loud wailing sound coming from somewhere in the distance. After shaking off our sleepy stupor, and remembering where we were and what we were doing there, we tried to figure out what it was that had so rudely awakened us after only five hours of sleep. We finally figured out that it was the sound of the *muezzin* (crier) of a mosque, calling faithful Muslims to prayer. We later determined that this mosque was across the highway from us, only about three hundred yards away from our house. Eventually, we would become accustomed to the *muezzin's* cry, and it no longer woke us, but for now, it was quite a wake up call, both literally and figuratively!

Another trademark sound of the city soon greeted us. Later in the day, as we were finishing lunch, a faint roaring sound began to approach. The sound grew increasingly loud until it became deafening, shaking the entire house. When we looked out the window, we were greeted by the sight of a column of U.S. tanks and armored personnel carriers, on their way back to the American military base that was only a few miles from our house. "Well," we said to each other, "At least they are our guys!"

As the roar of the armored column faded into the distance, we experienced a third sound that we would hear often over the next year: *clippity clop, clippity clop, clippity clop.* A glance out the window revealed this to be a ubiquitous feature of Tuzla: a horse-drawn cart. After all this, Jennifer and I asked each other, "What kind of place is this? What have we done?" We had truly come to a land of contrasts. We saw Mercedes Benzes, tanks, and horse-drawn carts. Great mansions and totally burned-out and leveled houses. People filled with hate, others filled with joy due to their relationship with Christ, and everything in between.

At first we felt fortunate, because at least our living conditions were not as difficult as the might have been. For example, people who lived in the city limits and who had city water only had it from about 4:00 in the afternoon to about 8:00 in the morning due to the damage that the war had inflicted on the water system. They had to keep their bathtubs filled with water for the "down" times. The house we were renting, however, was just outside of town, and our water came from an underground spring, meaning that we had water around the clock. This was great – until the summer, when the hot, dry weather caused the spring to start drying up. By July, the water coming out of our taps was little more than a trickle, and we had to start getting most of our water from an outdoor spring (which for some reason never dried up). Showers were impossible. If we wanted a hot bath, we had to fill up a kettle with water from the bottles we kept it in, heat it on our stove, and pour it in the tub. For the first time in my life, I understood the meaning of the phrase "drawing a bath!"

Even when the weather cooled and we again had water flowing through our pipes, the color of the water varied from rust to whitish to (occasionally) clear. Even the local residents marveled at the poor quality of our water. Once a Bosnian friend of ours turned on the tap and filled up a glass with water. It looked more like milk. He said to us, "What is this, some kind of joke?!?" It wasn't. We explained that this was how our water looked most of the time. We tried using a filter, but it would get clogged up after only a few uses. So, we gave up and eventually went back to getting our drinking water from the outdoor spring. Why the outdoor spring never dried up, we had no idea; we were just thankful that it didn't. We certainly learned never to take water for granted any more! As we had when we had moved to Prague, we eventually adapted and learned to pace ourselves and to adjust our expectations to our new way of life.

Ministry in Tuzla

We found, however, that adjusting to the challenges of daily life was nothing compared to dealing with the problems that we faced in our ministry. One source of opposition that we faced was, ironically, the Tuzla Baptist Church itself. When we agreed to move to Tuzla, we were told that our evangelistic ministry would be twofold. First, we would support the existing Baptist church, which was largely self-functioning, except that they did not have a regular preacher. I quickly became their main preacher. Even when they had someone else preaching (always another missionary, some local and some from out of town), I led the singing and played guitar.

The members of the church were enthusiastic and sincere in their beliefs, but working with the couple who were the two main lay leaders proved to be difficult. They had suffered persecution during the war and were still struggling with the after effects. The husband, a Serb, had once been seized by a group of masked Muslim militiamen, taken with several other Serbs several miles outside of town, and told that the whole group was to be "executed." Miraculously, he and several others were later released with no explanation. Not long after we began working with them, we found that we had inadvertently offended them in several ways, by doing things such as not inviting them to our house within a week or so of our arrival. It took us a while to realize that Bosnian people are extremely hospitable and constantly have friends and relatives over. To not invite someone over when meeting them is a great insult. When we tried to explain that we did not mean anything by our slights, they found it hard believe us. Before long, we were told that we were no longer welcome to attend their church. Thankfully, after several months, they forgave us, and I was soon preaching there again.

Both before, during, and after our time of "exile" from the Tuzla Baptist Church, we carried out the second major part of our ministry: leading several loosely connected home Bible studies that had been formed before we came and guiding them toward becoming house churches. Overall, this was a positive experience; still, the groups never really grew, and finding lay leaders proved nearly impossible. This ministry was also a source of contention between us and the Baptist church, for two main reasons. First, the Baptist church did not believe that there should be any other churches in town (and actually, they were probably right!). Second, there was some bad blood between members of the church and members of the Bible studies that went back well into the war and even beyond.

We also encountered problems with Muslim fundamentalists. At one evangelistic program that I and several of my colleagues (other missionaries who had arrived after us) conducted, a group of young Muslims sat through the program until the very end. At that time, they fanned out across the room, whipped out their Korans, and began preaching to the crowd. Almost no one stayed to listen, but the few who did actively debated with the preachers. Thankfully, there was no violence.

On another occasion, we hosted a volunteer group from the United States whose main ministry was conducting a medical clinic. One of the volunteers, a sweet elderly lady, asked if she could tell Bible stories to the children of those who came to the clinic. We arranged for her to tell the stories via a translator on a plaza just outside the hotel. About twenty or so children came, and they listened enthusiastically. I was also among the listeners, and I noticed that during the stories, an increasing number of grown men began to crowd around. Unlike the children, these new members of the audience were not smiling. They began to get closer and closer to the storyteller, and their expressions became increasingly angry. Finally, a man with a long beard, who happened to be a local imam, started shouting at us. He told the children to leave; they should not be listening to these stories! The crowd quickly dispersed, and some of the other missionaries and I whisked the storyteller away so that there would be no trouble. Again, we were thankful that there had been no violence.

Although we faced plenty of difficulties during our time in Tuzla, we also enjoyed many joyful experiences. We forged strong bonds of friendships with both missionaries and nationals. We saw the faith of many Bosnian Christians strengthened, and we even saw a few embrace the faith for the first time. One of the most exciting and enjoyable ministries we had was my baseball ministry. Once while I was jogging, a young man came up to me and asked in English, "Do you know the rules to baseball?" "Of course!" I replied, "It's my favorite sport!" As we jogged on together, he explained that a group of U. S. soldiers had once come into town with some baseball equipment and taught him and some of his friends to play. They had been able to return, however, and since that time, my new young friend had been looking for someone to help him and his "team" learn to play better.

I eagerly accepted this invitation and soon I was teaching and playing baseball with a dozen or so boys aged between fifteen and eighteen years old. I found some of their misconceptions about the rules to be amusing; for example, they believed that to put a runner out, you had to hit him with the ball! Soon, however, they stopped throwing balls at runners and learned the numerous rules of the game. They now needed some equipment. Through the generosity of some nearby soldiers and some churches in the States, I was able to donate a great deal of equipment to them. I also helped them with their English skills and spent hours discussing all types of issues with them. Most importantly, I was able to share my faith with them; two even told me that they wanted to become followers of Jesus. The baseball players were constantly in our home, eating brownies and other goodies that Jennifer made, watching American movies with us, and discussing Christianity. As long as I live, I will never forget those young men and will treasure the great times we had together.

Another blessing we experienced during our time in Tuzla was the relationship we had with our language tutor and translator, whom I will call Jelena. Jelena was kind and patient and proved invaluable in helping us to understand not only the language, but also Bosnian culture and history. She also helped us get out of several jams. Once when we were driving to visit some colleagues in another city, we passed through another town and were stopped by the police. Without explaining why, they demanded that we follow them to the local police station. Once we arrived there, they took our passports and made us sit in the waiting area of the station. The officers disappeared and were gone for several minutes. We were starting to worry about what might happen to us. When the police returned, Jelena negotiated with the police for several minutes. After several minutes of loud, heated discussion, they returned our passports and told us we could go. Needless to say, we were greatly relieved and grateful to Jelena for her help!

Jelena was very interested in God and the Bible. She faithfully attended nearly every Bible study that I led and served as translator most of the time. Jennifer and I frequently discussed God, Christ, the Bible and the Church with her. It was clear to us that Jelena loved both God and the Scriptures. Because of this, I thought that it would no problem to convert her to the Baptist faith. But she would have no part of leaving the Orthodox Church. I could not understand why she was so loyal to what seemed to me to be an antiquated, tradition-encrusted religious tradition...until a few years later, when I would come to fully understand.

Soon, our two-year term drew to a close. In the months prior to our departure date, we began thinking, praying, and seeking God's direction. Where would we go next, and what would we do?

Chapter Five: Intermission

Come to Me, all you who labor and are heavy laden, and I will give you rest.
— MATTHEW 11:28

Departure

As we began to think about what to do once our two-year mission term was over, we sensed no clear direction from God. At first, feeling the great weight of all the stressors that we had experienced, we thought that we might take a break from full-time missions service. I began to consider returning to seminary and working on a Doctor of Ministry degree for a couple of years, after which we would return to the mission field. After a little more time, prayer, and thought, I remembered a spiritual principle that I had once learned (and which I still believe): When you are seeking God's will on what to do next, and you receive no answer, keep doing what you are currently doing until you hear otherwise. We were sure that we had been called into long-term missionary service, and we did not sense that we should move in a different direction at that time. With that in mind, we began the process of applying to return to the field as long-term career missionaries. The next question, of course, was where to go. We looked at several possibilities, including Belgrade, Serbia, and even a city in Poland. But soon, we became aware of a third possibility.

When we had been in missionary training, we had become friends with another young couple who were on their way to Moscow. We had kept in touch with them while we were in Prague. A few months after we transferred to Tuzla, we were delighted to find out that our friends were also transferring to Bosnia – to the nearby city of Banja Luka. Unlike Tuzla, which was in the predominantly Muslim part of Bosnia, Banja Luka was in the Serb-controlled part. We kept in close touch with our friends, visiting them when we could, and hosting them on other occasions. They constantly told us of the spiritual openness of the people of Banja Luka. They had been able to lead many people to make professions of faith, and they even baptized a few. Still, these new converts were unwilling to actually join the tiny Baptist church in Banja Luka. Instead, they remained loyal to the Orthodox Church.

By this time, our mission board had several short-term personnel in Banja Luka, but no career missionaries. As we considered the possibility of living and working there long-term, we realized that although we knew and loved people from all three of the major ethnic groups in Bosnia, we felt the closest bond with the Serbs. This was partly true because of all the nationalities in Bosnia, the Serbs seemed to be the most interested in the Gospel. Still, we were concerned with how the Orthodox hierarchy might react to our presence in Banja Luka. We had heard horror stories (most of which turned out to be greatly exaggerated) about anti-evangelical statements made and actions taken by Orthodox clergy throughout the Serb lands, and so the idea of working as evangelical missionaries in that environment was a little intimidating.

However, after I had a meeting with the pastor of the Orthodox parish in Tuzla, my concerns were allayed. He assured me that although there were some radical nationalists among the clergy (mainly in a part of the country far from Banja Luka), most Orthodox priests and bishops were decent people. I resolved then and there that I would not attempt to try and persuade pious Orthodox believers to leave the Church, but rather to reach people who were not involved in church. Indeed, this decision agreed with the practice of all of all our personnel.

So, we decided to "re-up," becoming career missionaries who would minister among the Serbs in Banja Luka. Future events would seem to indicate that God was definitely behind our decision to work with the Serbs.

Rest & Refitting

Near the end of April 1998, we flew back to the States. After a couple of months living with our parents, we moved into a missionary house owned by a large Baptist church in northeast Houston. We spent our time there resting, visiting family and friends, speaking in various churches about our time in Bosnia, and preparing for the birth of our second child. This new baby arrived on September 4, 1998. She was another beautiful girl whom we named Courtney.

The next month, we headed to our mission board's training center for two months of training. The center was located in a beautiful, peaceful, and quiet rural setting near Richmond, Virginia. There we both attended classes and studied on our own to prepare for our next assignment. We knew that we would be working with a people who were traditionally Orthodox, so we began studying a little about Orthodoxy. I reread *The Orthodox Church* by Bishop Kallistos Ware, this time more slowly and carefully. I also read a booklet by Archbishop Dmitri of Dallas about basic Orthodox beliefs. Because the Archbishop's pamphlet was out of print, I made a Xerox copy of the entire thing. In my copy, I carefully highlighted each part where Orthodox doctrines differed from my own beliefs. I found that although there were significant differences, at least seventy-five percent of Orthodox beliefs seemed to agree with those laid out in *The Baptist Faith and Message*, the official doctrinal statement of the Southern Baptist Convention.

The most significant encounter that Jennifer and I had with Orthodoxy that fall was when we had the opportunity to visit an Orthodox parish. We had attended one Divine Liturgy two years before when we had been in training for our first missionary term. However, the parish we attended was a Greek church, and at least half of the service was in Greek and therefore unintelligible to us. That Sunday had happened to be a day when the parish was holding its annual Greek festival, and we enjoyed visiting the various craft booths and eating the delicious food. I remember one man telling us, "We are the oldest Christian church in the whole world." I also remember that as much as I would have liked to, I could not argue with him on that point.

This time, we were assigned the task of taking a trip to St. Nicholas Cathedral in Washington, D. C. Unfortunately, we were not able to attend a Divine Liturgy, because we could only travel there on a weekday. Instead, the dean of the cathedral, Fr. Constantine White, spoke to us about Orthodoxy and showed us around the church. He was very patient in answering our questions and very persuasive, particularly in explaining the meaning and function of icons. Before speaking with Fr. Constantine, I, like most evangelicals, assumed that having icons in church was tantamount to idolatry. Fr. Constantine convinced me that they have value in teaching the Gospel story in pictures and reminding us of the "great cloud of witnesses" that surround us and worship with us in heaven. He also explained that icons had been a part of Christian worship since at least the second century, and probably since the first. I had walked into the church anti-icon but had left with a positive view of them.

When our training was over, we returned to our temporary home and began packing and preparing for our trip to Banja Luka. After years of preparation, we were finally about to attain our dream of being career missionaries. We were ready to stay in Bosnia for many, many years and minister to the Serb people. We were finally about to "arrive." At least that is what we thought!

Chapter Six: Return

Eye has not seen, nor ear heard,
Nor have entered into the heart of man
The things which God has prepared for those who love Him.
— 1 CORINTHIANS 2:8

Banja Luka

We flew into Sarajevo in January of 1999, with our seven-year-old and our four-month-old in tow. From the airport, we took a van to our mission's Sarajevo headquarters, where half of our things were loaded into another van, and then we and our guides immediately began the drive to Banja Luka. It was evening, and a fairly heavy snow was falling. Between the darkness, the snow, and our unfamiliarity with the curving, mountainous road, it was a slow and grueling trip. Thankfully, we were following someone who knew the way. After several hours, we reached our temporary apartment in Banja Luka, where we unloaded our things and collapsed, exhausted.

Our temporary apartment was a truly depressing place. It was on the top floor (essentially the attic) of a four-story house, each floor of which had been made into a separate apartment. All the rooms of our apartment except the central one had ceilings that sloped down, making it impossible for an adult, especially a tall one like me, to stand in half the room. To enter the kitchen, we actually had to leave the apartment! The lack of lighting and insulation made it constantly cold and dark. Some colleagues of ours who had lived in it before said that it was also unbearably hot in the summer. We resolved to get out of there as soon as we could!

After a couple of weeks' searching, we found a three-bedroom apartment on the ground floor of a much newer and nicer house. It was several miles from the center of town, but since we had a car, this was not much of a problem. Interestingly, every time we traveled to or from the center of town, we passed right by the Bosnian headquarters of the

International Orthodox Christian Charities. We had no idea that this fine organization would eventually be one of the main charities that we would support.

We soon found a school for Audrey and language tutors for ourselves, and we made friends with the other members of our missionary team and with the nationals with whom we would be working. Still, life was hard for the first couple of months. There was always a foot of snow on the ground, with plenty of ice thrown in as a bonus. This made driving around, and even walking, a challenge. For the third time in the last two and a half years, we had to get used to a new city, new people, a new culture, and so on. By the first of March, however, we felt that we had turned a corner – we were going to make it!

But just as we had begun to feel comfortable in Banja Luka, an uprising broke out in Kosovo. When the government of Yugoslavia sent troops into Kosovo to suppress the rebellion, NATO decided to bomb Yugoslavia to try and bring its military activities to an end. When the advance warning of the bombing was given, our organization decided to evacuate all of our missionaries that were living in Serb lands – two families in Belgrade plus the three families and two singles in Banja Luka. Although Banja Luka was not bombed, our supervisors felt that there might be reprisals against Americans, and they wanted to take no chances. We had only a few hours to pack. With great sadness, we gathered as many things as we could fit in our car, and left the home that we had quickly grown to love, not knowing when or even if we would return.

Redeployment

We joined all of the other missionary evacuees in a hotel in Croatia, where we spent a week grieving, praying, and talking with our colleagues and supervisors about where we might go, since Banja Luka was no longer an option. We were determined to one day return to Banja Luka, so we decided that it would be best to go to another part of Bosnia, where we could continue studying the language. Although Tuzla seemed like an obvious place to go, we felt that there would be too much pressure to immediately get involved in ministry, and our language learning would suffer. Finally, we decided to go to Sarajevo. To be exact, we would settle in the suburb of Ilidza, which had been predominantly inhabited by Serbs before the war and which still had a significant Serb population.

When we arrived in Sarajevo around the first of April, 1999, we were totally unprepared for what we saw there. Whereas Tuzla and Banja Luka had suffered little damage during the war, Sarajevo had been the site of some of the worst fighting. During the four-year long war, parts of Sarajevo had changed sides dozens of times. As we drove around the city, we stared in utter disbelief as we saw entire neighborhoods that had been reduced to mere rubble. Graveyards with hundreds of new graves were ubiquitous. It seemed as if a perpetual dark cloud hung over the city, along with a spirit of deep, dark depression. Once again, we asked ourselves what on earth we were doing here! And once again, for the fourth time in three years, we struggled with culture shock and mild depression.

We soon found a nice house in which to stay and immersed ourselves in language study. We did nothing but study the language for several months, because we wanted to be completely fluent by the time we returned to Banja Luka, even though we had to idea when that would be. Between the thirteen months that we had spent in Tuzla and the several months of intensive, immersion language study that we did during our first several months in Sarajevo, we became essentially fluent in the Bosnian/Serbian language. By the end of the year, I was able to lead Bible studies entirely in Bosnian, which greatly enhanced our ministry.

In the fall of our first year in Sarajevo, we began teaching English as a Second Language at our organization's educational center. This center had been established as a means to build relationships with people and hopefully give us opportunities to share the Gospel. One day in December, as I was walking home from my last class, the tiny snowflakes falling from the sky and the crunching sound coming from under my feet told me that it had begun to snow. This was no surprise, for it had snowed many times before that day. What made this snow different was that it did not stop for several days. In fact, the snow did not stop until we had about two feet worth. Then it did stop for a day or so, which gave me enough time to shovel our walk.

Soon the snow began to fall again, and again it did not stop for several days. By the time the snow had finally stopped for good, we had no less than four feet on the ground! Needless to say, we Texas natives had no prior experience in dealing with so much snow. Our car was completely buried, and even if it had not been, it took nearly a week for the roads to be clear enough to drive on. So, if we needed food or anything else, we simply put on our snow boots and trudged through the snow until we had what we needed. Thankfully, we did not lose water or power for more than a few hours at a time. I will never forget the sight of all that snow, which in places was piled up over my head, and which took about three months to completely melt.

While in Sarajevo, I met a devout Orthodox Serb named Vladimir. One Sunday morning, I went with him to the Divine Liturgy at his church, known popularly as the "Old Orthodox Church." Old it was indeed; while the majority of the structure dated from the 18th century, parts of it were actually built in the sixth century. Unfortunately, the service did not make much of an impression on me, partly because we arrived very late, and I could not understand most of the service. Still, it was an honor to be in such an old and historic church.

Vladimir was very interested both in studying the Bible and in learning English. I went to his apartment about once a week to read and discuss the Bible with him in Bosnian and in English. We had a great many discussions about God, Christ, the Bible and the Church. It was obvious that Vladimir loved both God and the Scriptures, and that he was fully dedicated to following Christ in all areas of his life. Because of this, I thought that it would be easy to persuade him to become a Baptist and to join a Baptist church. But, in spite of his deep faith in Jesus, Vladimir had no interest in leaving the Orthodox

Church. His stubborn dedication to the Church of his upbringing frustrated me, as had Jelena's a couple of years before. And yet, their loyalty to Orthodoxy made an impression on me that would later prompt me to do some deep reflection of my own on the Orthodox Church.

The rest of our time in Sarajevo was relatively uneventful. We taught a few more English classes, and I led a few Bible studies and even preached once in a local church (in Bosnian, but closely following a manuscript!), but we mainly just continued studying the language. In November of 1999, one of our colleagues who had lived in Belgrade before the bombing was offered the opportunity to move to Banja Luka. He accepted the offer, and I helped him move. This was my first time to be in Banja Luka in eight months. It was wonderful to be back! Nothing seemed to have changed. Although we too could have moved back then, we decided to wait until the school year was over, for Audrey's sake. She was attending a local public school (having become completely fluent in the language), and we felt it was important for her to be able to finish a whole school year in one place, for the first time in her life.

Finally, in late July, it was time to return to our beloved adopted city of Banja Luka. After yet another long delay, we were about to "arrive": we would finally be in the place we wanted to be, doing what we wanted to be doing, and able to speak the language. After years of preparation and moving around, we were ready to settle down in one place and stay there for a long time. I am sure that God must have been laughing as we were having those thoughts!

Starting Over

I am frequently asked: "Why did you go to preach the Gospel to the Serbs? After all, aren't they a Christian people?" The correct answer to this question is "yes and no." It is indisputable that the overwhelming number of Serbs *consider* themselves to be Orthodox Christians. Still, most of these are Christian (and Orthodox, I might add) in name only. In fact, of all the peoples of Eastern Europe, the Serbs rank near the bottom in the percent that attend church regularly. Only a small percentage of Serbs possess the living and active faith that the Orthodox Church teaches is necessary for salvation.

So, our aim was not to try to turn any pious, active Orthodox believers (of whom there were relatively few in Banja Luka) into Baptists. Our goal was rather to find people who were not active in church, share the gospel as we understood it with them, hopefully persuade them to accept baptism (in the Baptist fashion), and begin attending either the local Baptist church or at least a small-group Bible study.

Yes, you read correctly! There actually was a tiny Baptist group in Banja Luka that called itself a church. It had always had only about five active members, with a few other occasional attenders, and was led by a young couple from Serbia. The husband served as the pastor, and I soon became the music leader by default, as I was the only attender who could play an instrument. The service consisted of a brief opening prayer, a few songs led by me as I played my guitar, another prayer, a Scripture reading or two, a sermon of about forty-five minutes to an hour, and a closing prayer. Occasionally, a guest or two from out of town would give a testimony. The services were held on Sunday afternoon, because the group was renting the space owned by another evangelical church. The space was a small room with completely white walls. In short, the Baptist services were worlds apart from an Orthodox Liturgy.

In addition to working with the Baptist group, I also did whatever I could to build relationships with locals, with a view toward sharing the Gospel with them. This I did with gusto. I was able to spend a great deal of time in homes, cafes, shops, and elsewhere, talking with people about God, Jesus, the Bible, church, and salvation. I had never enjoyed a job more. I quickly made many new friends and had many fruitful conversations. Most of my new friends listened politely, and many even agreed with much of what I said. Still, I saw no conversions.

We were blessed to be able to work as a team with

another couple, whom I will call Bob and Melanie. They had served in Belgrade before the NATO bombing and had moved around several times before having been given the opportunity to move to Banja Luka a few months before we did. They were beautiful people, and we became fast friends. Bob and I met once a week to plan and strategize, and all four of us met another time during the week to pray, read Scripture, and fellowship together. We also took turns leading a brief devotional.

One time, when it was my turn to lead the devotional, I chose as my text 1 Corinthians. 9:19-22:

> For though I am free from all men, I have made myself a servant to all, that I might win the more; and to the Jews I became as a Jew, that I might win Jews; to those who are under the law, as under the law, that I might win those who are under the law; to those who are without law, as without law…that I might win those who are without law; to the weak I became as weak, that I might win the weak. I have become all things to all men, that I might by all means save some.

I discussed the fact that our organization had spent a great deal of money and manpower trying to build up the Baptist church in Banja Luka (no fewer than twelve adult missionaries had each spent six to eighteen months ministering there prior to our arrival)…but with little to show for it. Our missionaries had been able to lead people to make professions of faith in Christ, and had even baptized a few. But when they had challenged people to join the Baptist church, virtually no one had been willing. They were unwilling to leave the Orthodox tradition.

I surmised that the problem may have been that our predecessors had perhaps been "too Baptist." I suggested that if we could "become all things to all men," which in our case meant being as Orthodox as possible while still remaining faithful to Baptist principles, we might be more successful. How exactly we were to do this, I was not sure. But all four of us agreed that this was a good idea, and we all decided to take it under consideration. Clearly, however, the first step was to become more educated about Orthodoxy.

This devotional prompted me to entertain another thought. I asked myself, "What is it about this faith that inspires such loyalty? Few of the people here ever darken the door of a church, and yet they will not leave their tradition. In fact, many have been willing to fight and die for it!" While thinking about this, I recalled my experience with Jelena and Vladimir, who had refused to leave Orthodoxy despite my efforts to persuade them to do so. I resolved right then and there to study more about the Orthodox faith and see if I could solve this mystery.

I still had my copy of *The Orthodox Church* by Bishop Kallistos and my pamphlet by Archbishop Dmitri on the basics of Orthodoxy. I reread them both and thought, "Well, that was interesting. We Baptists really have more in common with the Orthodox Church than I had thought!" Many of the Orthodox practices that had seemed so bizarre and "unbiblical" now made a little more sense, even if I still did not agree with them.

Unfortunately, however, I had nothing else to read on Orthodoxy, at least not in English (I wasn't quite ready to try to read any theological works in Serbian!). Then one day I received a phone call from Melanie. She said, "James, I have a book here that you might find interesting."

I had absolutely no idea that this book would totally and irrevocably change my life!

Dangerous Reading

I asked Melanie, "What is the book about?" She replied, "It is about a group of men that used to work for Campus Crusade for Christ but who all converted to Orthodoxy." I thought to myself, "Why on earth would anyone want to do that?" I just had to read the book and find out.

What really caught my attention about this book was the fact that it was not just about Protestants converting to

Orthodoxy, nor even just about Evangelicals converting. I had heard stories before about both of these types of conversions. What amazed me was that the book was about a group of leaders of Campus Crusade for Christ converting. Campus Crusade is an evangelical organization devoted primarily to evangelizing college students. Nearly all evangelical missionaries, myself included, held Campus Crusade in high esteem; its workers we practically viewed as saints. In our thinking, they ranked right up there with missionaries and martyrs in the evangelical "hall of fame."

So now I was being told that not only did Orthodoxy inspire great loyalty among the Serbs and other Eastern Europeans, but it had also attracted some of the most dedicated American evangelical Christians in the world. Needless to say, I had to find out what these high ranking leaders of an esteemed evangelical ministry, along with two thousand of their followers, found so persuasive about the ancient faith.

The book that Melanie mentioned is *Becoming Orthodox*, by Fr. Peter Gillquist. It is a quick, easy read, and the story it narrates is gripping. I read the book in one day. After I finished it, I remember thinking, "Gillquist raises some interesting points, but I'm not sold." I was not able to reject his arguments outright, but neither could I immediately accept them. So, for a while I put the book aside and tried to forget about what I had read. I tried to just go on with my life and ministry. It didn't work.

Chapter Seven: The New Testament Church

And they continued steadfastly in the apostles' doctrine and
fellowship, in the breaking of bread, and in prayers.
—ACTS 2:42

Despite my attempts to forget what I had read in *Becoming Orthodox*, I could not get Fr. Peter's arguments out of my head. I began to grow increasingly confused as to exactly what I believed. To help me clarify my thinking, I decided to reread the book. This time, I spent a whole day reading through it slowly and carefully. After this second read, I became convinced of several truths about the early Christian Church, all of which flew in the face of what I had been taught in seminary and in the various churches I had attended.

All of my pastors and seminary professors had taught me that the Baptist church, despite its many imperfections, was nevertheless one of the most, if not the most, faithful reproductions of the Church that the Apostles had founded. Accordingly, my Baptist friends and colleagues and I prided ourselves on being part of a "New Testament Church," that is, a church modeled after the primitive, first-century Church seen in the pages of the New Testament. We felt that if a person could go back in time and visit a Christian worship service in the days of the Apostles, he would be amazed to find that it was nearly exactly like...well, a Baptist service! If this time-traveler were to have a long discussion with Peter, James, Paul, and John, he would find that their views on theology, church government, and liturgical practice would be nearly identical to those of the Baptists and other evangelicals. After all, our theology and practice were all clearly taught by the Bible. Or were they?

My readings of *Becoming Orthodox* showed me that these and many other assumptions, which I had held for so many years, were based neither on the history of the early Church nor on Scripture. In particular, Fr. Peter changed my mind on four key points regarding the early Church's worship style, its view of sacraments, its polity, and its view of Scripture and Tradition.

The Early Church was Liturgical

I had always been taught that early Christian worship services were more or less spontaneous, with little structure, and I had never questioned this teaching. Moreover, my years in the Episcopal Church had turned me off to any type of liturgical structure. I had come to believe that any service that came out of a book and that was basically the same from week to week was dry, dead, and boring. Surely the worship of the first and second century Church, which all Christians saw as a dynamic and exciting "Golden Age," could not have looked anything like the liturgical routine practiced by the most traditional churches!

And yet, on further examination, I saw plenty of evidence that liturgical worship was not an erroneous practice that crept into the Church two or three hundred years after Jesus' death. Instead, it was an integral part of the Church's adoration of God from the beginning. I had long understood that the very first members of the Church did not see themselves as founders of a new religion but rather simply as Jews who had found the Messiah. But what I had never realized before was that the Apostles and other early Christians had continued the same worship practices that they had followed as Jews, including worshipping in the synagogues and praying in the Temple, at least until they were thrown out.

In Acts 2:42, a verse much loved by evangelical church planters like myself, we read "And they (i.e., the early Christians) continued steadfastly in the apostles' doctrine and fellowship, in the breaking of bread, and in prayers." I had never before realized that the Greek word usually translated as "prayers" or even "prayer" in most Protestant translations is *tais proseuchais*, or "the prayers." In other words, the Christians were not merely being steadfast in prayer in general; rather, they were being steadfast in saying the prayers; that is, the specific liturgical prayers said by all Jews using fixed words at fixed times during the day. We see this further confirmed in the next chapter, when we read that "Peter and John went up together to the temple at the hour of prayer, the ninth hour" (Acts 3:1).

Another evidence for the presence of liturgical worship in the early Church is found in the account of the worship service in Antioch that led to the sending of Ss. Paul and Barnabas on the first missionary journey. In the thirteenth chapter of Acts, St. Luke writes "As they (the church in Antioch) ministered to the Lord and fasted, the Holy Spirit said, 'Now separate to Me Barnabas and Saul for the work to which I have called them'" (v. 2). Here the Greek word rendered "ministered" ("worshipped" in the New International Version), is a form of *leitourgeo*, from which the English word "liturgy" derives. In other words, the church of Antioch was literally conducting a liturgy!

The *Orthodox Study Bible* sheds more light on the word leiturgeo:

> [The word] means "to perform ritual acts: Literally translated, this passage would read "As they liturgized to the Lord and fasted." Liturgical worship did not originate in Antioch. The Christians in Antioch were taught how to worship by Saul and Barnabas (11:22, 25, 26). It is in the midst of this liturgy that the Holy Spirit speaks.[2]

The idea of the Holy Spirit actually speaking through any type of liturgy was inconceivable to me; but there it was in the Bible, in a passage that I loved dearly! For someone who thought so highly of the early Church but so lowly of liturgical worship, all this was a hard pill to swallow.

Of course, the early Church did not merely continue Jewish liturgical practice unaltered. As we see in both the Scriptures and early extra-biblical Christian writings, the

---

[2] *The Orthodox Study Bible: New Testament and Psalms*, New King James Version (Nashville: Thomas Nelson, 1993), 299.

Apostles and their followers combined the elements of the synagogue liturgy, including hymns, prayers, and one or more sermons, with something new: the *agape* (love) feast. The latter was a fellowship meal that included a second service called the Eucharist. The latter consisted of hymns, prayers of thanksgiving and worship, and a commemoration of the Last Supper. Within a generation of the founding of the Church, however, due to the Church's rapid growth and to improper conduct during the meal in some places (see 1 Cor. 11:17-34), the fellowship meal was removed from the main worship service, leaving the first part (the *synaxis* or Liturgy of the Word) and the Eucharist.

Additionally, the earliest extra-biblical witnesses confirm the liturgical nature of the early Church's worship. Writing around 150 A.D., or only about fifty years after the death of the Apostle John, St. Justin the Philosopher (known to most Protestants and Catholics as "Justin Martyr") gives the earliest description of the Church's worship structure in an oft quoted passage that bears repeating:

> [O]n the day called Sunday, all who live in cities or in the country gather together to one place, and the memoirs of the apostles or the writings of the prophets are read, as long as time permits; then, when the reader has ceased, the president verbally instructs, and exhorts to the imitation of these good things. Then we all rise together and pray, and, as we before said, when our prayer is ended, bread and wine and water are brought, and the president in like manner offers prayers and thanksgivings, according to his ability, and the people assent, saying Amen; and there is a distribution to each, and a participation of that over which thanks have been given, and to those who are absent a portion is sent by the deacons. And they who are well to do, and willing, give what each thinks

fit; and what is collected is deposited with the president.[3]

There I was, faced with clear evidence, both in the Bible and within two generations of the close of the apostolic age, that Christian worship followed a twofold liturgical pattern, including a Liturgy of the Word, and a weekly celebration of the Eucharist. On further reflection, the presence of liturgical worship in ancient Christianity was not all that surprising. For when I was truly honest with myself, I had to admit that even Baptist worship, whether "contemporary" or "traditional," is no more spontaneous or unplanned than Orthodox services; it merely follows an unwritten plan rather than a service book. Nearly all evangelical services follow a similar pattern: a mixture of prayers, hymns or praise choruses, testimonies in speech or in song, and Scripture readings, followed by a somewhat lengthy sermon, which is usually the centerpiece of the service. In short, the pattern is similar to that which St. Justin described, but with a lengthened sermon taking the place of the Eucharist. In the end, I had to admit that I, like nearly all evangelicals, had always believed in a type of liturgical service. "So," I thought, "Why should I not begin to participate in the type of liturgy that the earliest Christians practiced?"

The Early Church was Hierarchical

"A New Testament church of the Lord Jesus Christ is an autonomous local congregation of baptized believers.... Its scriptural officers are pastors and deacons." (The Baptist Faith and Message, 2000 revision, Article 6)[4]

The Baptist Faith and Message ("BFM" for short) is a doctrinal statement published by the Southern Baptist

---

[3] St. Justin the Philosopher, *First Apology*, Ch. 62, in Alexander Roberts and James Donaldson, eds., *The Ante-Nicene Fathers, Volume 1: The Apostolic Fathers, Justin Martyr, Irenaeus*, fourth printing (Peabody, MA: Hendrickson, 2004), 186.

[4] Obtained from the following web page: http://www.sbc.net/bfm/bfm2000.asp.

Convention. The overwhelming majority of Southern Baptists accept it, and all Southern Baptist missionaries, seminary professors, and denominational officials are required to sign a statement saying that they agree with it. I had always thought it strange that a denomination that believed in the complete sufficiency of the Bible for all things related to Christian doctrine and practice found it necessary to produce a statement of doctrine to supplement and clarify Scripture. Like my co-religionists, however, I had accepted it as a "necessary evil," because many Christians (even some Baptists) who claimed to follow the Bible alone ended up believing or practicing things that seemed to be at odds with the plain teaching of Scripture, at least as I understood it.

I had always accepted the Baptist teaching on church leadership without question. I knew that the New Testament uses three words for church leaders: *episkopos* (literally "overseer," but traditionally translated as "bishop"), *presbyteros* (literally "elder", but often transliterated as "presbyter"), and *diakonos* ("minister" or "deacon"). However, as my pastors and professors had taught me, I held that the first two terms were used interchangeably. So in my thinking, as the BFM stated, the Church's "scriptural officers are pastors and deacons." I had no place for the idea of a ruling or "monarchical" bishop who gives orders to the other ministers, even the presbyters.

But an experience that I had early in my journey toward Orthodoxy convinced me that perhaps I had misunderstood the Scriptures' witness about the nature of church leadership. Soon after arriving in Banja Luka, I began leading an intensive Bible study on the book of Acts for a couple of members of the Baptist church. One day, the day on which we were to study the Jerusalem Council in Acts 15, only one of my students was able to come. He was a very devout young man whom I shall call David. Of all of my Serb friends in Banja Luka, David was the one to whom I felt the closest.

In Acts 15, we see the Apostles and the other leaders of the Church gathered to discuss a critical issue that had arisen as a result of St. Paul's first missionary journey. The problem before them was, in essence: Did Gentiles converting to Christianity have to first become Jews, or could they be received directly into Christianity, without first being circumcised or submitting to the full Old Testament Law? As David and I were studying the text, we noticed that after the council discussed the issue at hand, St. James said, "Simon [i.e. St. Peter] has declared how God at the first visited the Gentiles to take out of them a people for His name. And with this the words of the prophets agree." Then, after quoting a passage from the Prophet Amos, he concludes, "Therefore, I judge that they should not trouble those from among the Gentiles who are turning to God, but that we write to them to abstain from things polluted by idols, from sexual immorality, from things strangled, and from blood" (Acts 15:14-15,19-20).

James' words "I judge" are key here. At the council, there was much discussion, during which at the very least Peter, Paul, and Barnabas spoke. But then all were silent, waiting for James to make a ruling. There was no vote, and after James ruled, there was no further discussion. Rather, the Scripture tells us that "it pleased the apostles and elders, with the whole church" (15:22) to send people out to the various churches with St. James and the council's ruling. As David and I said to each other "i to je bilo to!" (and that was that!).

I remember looking at David and saying, "That sounds like something a bishop would say and do." David looked at me and said, "Yes, it sure does." David and I, happy Baptists that we were, discovered on that day that the first century Church really did seem to have bishops that made rulings, just as the Orthodox Church has always taught. This experience definitely planted a seed in both David's and my mind. For the first time, I admitted that the idea that the early Church was hierarchical and not democratic and congregational, was not "unbiblical," but was actually firmly grounded in Scripture.

When I began to read the earliest extra-biblical writings, written by Church leaders who had sat at the feet of the Apostles and who carried on their ministry, I found that like the New Testament writers, the authors of the two earliest works also used the words *episkopos* and *presbyteros* interchangeably. The *Didache*, written around 100 A.D., speaks of bishops and deacons, while St. Clement, in his epistle to the church in Corinth, explicitly mentions only elders and deacons. However, Clement also alludes to the presence of a threefold ministry, most notably in the following passage:

> Those then who offer their sacrifices at the appointed seasons are acceptable and blessed; *for since they comply with the Master's orders*, they do no sin. Thus to the high priest have been appointed his proper services, to the priests, their own place assigned, upon the Levites their proper duties imposed, and the layman is bound by the rules for laymen (*emphasis added*).[5]

Clement is speaking not about Old Testament times, but about the Church of his day. It is hard to avoid the conclusion that the "high priest" refers to the *episkopos* or bishop of a congregation, the "priests" to the *presbyteroi*, the elders, and the "Levites" to the *diakonoi*, or deacons. This passage clearly shows that, at least in Rome, by 95 A.D., the Church already had a threefold ministry that was distinguished from that of the laity. Moreover, we see that these "high priests," "priests," and "Levites," in carrying out their ministries, do so on Christ's orders.

Moreover, it is an historical fact that is that the church in Antioch had a ruling bishop in place by no later than 70 A.D., which falls squarely within the New Testament age. His name was Ignatius, and the epistles that he wrote about forty years later contain some statements that I found shocking. Repeatedly, Ignatius speaks of deacons, presbyters, and bishops as three distinct offices, and he urges the churches of Asia Minor and Rome to obey their bishops in all things.

After reading all this, I had to ask myself the following question: Were my denomination and I right about the nature of early Church leadership? Were *episkopoi* non-monarchical?

---

[5] St. Clement of Rome, *Epistle to the Corinthians* (1 Clement), Ch. 40, in Fr. Jack Sparks, ed. *The Apostolic Fathers* (Minneapolis: Light and Life Publishing, 1978), 40.

Were they really just the same as *presbyteroi*? Or were the Orthodox and other hierarchical churches correct in saying that monarchical bishops had existed from the beginning? Was it true, as the Orthodox Church claimed, that each church had several *presbyteroi* and that the leader of this group was the *episkopos*, with whom the proverbial "buck" stopped? I could not deny that both the historical and biblical evidence favored the Orthodox position. When I had to choose between the Baptist position and that of Clement and Ignatius (not to mention other early writers such as St. Irenaeus of Lyons), I felt that I had to go with the men who had learned their doctrine and practice directly from the Apostles.

The Early Church Was Sacramental

"Christian baptism is…an act of obedience symbolizing the believer's faith in a crucified, buried, and risen Saviour, the believer's death to sin, the burial of the old life, and the resurrection to walk in newness of life in Christ Jesus. The Lord's Supper is a *symbolic act* of obedience whereby members of the church, through partaking of the bread and the fruit of the vine, memorialize the death of the Redeemer and anticipate His second coming." (The Baptist Faith and Message, 2000 revision, Article 7 [*emphasis added*])[6]

I found Fr. Peter's third major point about the early Church to be the most difficult to accept. As a committed evangelical, I strongly disagreed with any theology that smacked of sacramentalism. For me and my fellow Southern Baptists, the Bible clearly taught that God's grace was directly imparted to believers upon their profession of faith, without any intermediate means. In other words, baptism did not convey the forgiveness of sins, and the Lord's Supper (the Baptist term for Holy Communion or the Eucharist) did not in any way contain the real presence of Christ. Both "ordinances," as Baptists call these rituals, were merely

---

[6]http://www.sbc.net/bfm/bfm2000.asp.

symbolic acts of obedience, albeit acts commanded by Jesus and a fundamental part of Christian practice.

But after reading *Becoming Orthodox*, I discovered several Scriptural passages that taught that baptism and the Eucharist were much more than merely symbolic acts. First of all, at the Last Supper, Jesus plainly said, "This is My body…" and "This is My blood…" (Matt. 26:26, 27), not "This *symbolizes* my body and blood." On an earlier occasion, Jesus had told a crowd of people:

> Unless you eat the flesh of the Son of Man and drink His blood, you have no life in you. Whoever eats my flesh and drinks My blood has eternal life, and I will raise him up at the last day…He who eats My flesh and drinks My blood abides in Me, and I in him. (John 6:53-54, 56).

All of the Bible teachers whom I had heard and all the biblical commentaries that I had read taught that Jesus is speaking metaphorically in both of these passages. I had never thought about the inconsistency between this affirmation and the way that Baptists and other evangelicals pride themselves on interpreting the Bible literally. It finally occurred to me that the main reason I and my fellow Baptists abandoned our literal hermeneutic in interpreting these Eucharistic passages was because we had previously made up our minds that the Lord's Supper is wholly symbolic and that absolutely nothing beside faith could contribute to salvation. Jesus had to have been speaking metaphorically; otherwise, he would have been contradicting what we understood the rest of the Bible to say.[7] But how, I asked, did the Apostles and their disciples understand the Eucharist? In his First Epistle to the Corinthians, St. Paul asks, "The cup of blessing which we bless, is it not the communion of the blood of Christ? The

---

[7] After Jesus spoke these words, many of his followers were offended and left him. If Jesus had been speaking metaphorically, why did he not simply say so, and thus prevent so many from walking away? Why would his followers be so offended by his words if they were merely a metaphor?

bread which we break, is it not the communion of the body of Christ?" (1 Cor. 10:16). The Greek word translated "communion" is *koinonia*, which implies a real and intimate participation with something or someone, not just a symbolic act. Later in the same epistle, St. Paul warns the Corinthian church about improper practice of the Eucharist. He urges them to examine themselves before they partake of Communion, lest they bring judgment on themselves. Some have not done so, and "For this reason, many are weak and sick among you, and many sleep [i.e. have died]" (1 Cor. 11:30). For some reason, I had been blinded to an obvious implication of this latter teaching: It is extremely unlikely that anyone would get sick or die because of something that was nothing more than plain bread or wine (let alone grape juice).

Perhaps most shocking of all to me were the words of St. Ignatius, who not only served as the bishop of Antioch from about 70 to about 110 A. D., but who also had been a disciple of the Apostle John for many years. If St. John and the other Apostles had taught that the Eucharist was merely symbolic, then surely Ignatius would not have contradicted their teaching. Ignatius commanded the churches of Asia Minor not only to be obedient to their leaders, but to also break "one loaf, which is the medicine of immortality, the antidote which results not in dying but in living forever in Jesus Christ."[8] This was incontrovertible evidence that the post-apostolic Church, from at least as early as 110 A.D., held a sacramental view of the Eucharist. Had Ignatius misunderstood his teacher St. John's teaching and that of his apostolic colleagues? Or had the evangelicals and I?

The biblical case for a sacramental view of baptism was even stronger than it had been for the Eucharist. Again, Fr. Peter helped me to see Scripture passages that I had read dozens of times in a whole new light. Attempting to lay aside all that I had been taught about the meaning of these passages, I reread all the Scriptures dealing with baptism. In so doing, I

---

[8] St. Ignatius of Antioch, *Letter to the Ephesians*, Ch. 20, in Fr. Jack Sparks, ed. *The Apostolic Fathers*, (Minneapolis, Light and Life publishing, 1978), 84.

found several passages that imply that baptism is more than symbolic.

At the conclusion of his sermon on the day of Pentecost, St. Peter told the listening crowd, "Repent, and let every one of you be baptized in the name of Jesus Christ, for the remission of your sins; and you shall receive the gift of the Holy Spirit" (Acts 2:38). Previously, I had always skipped over the phrase "for the remission of your sins," but I now had to come to terms with these words. After St. Paul's conversion on the road to Damascus, Ananias said to him, "Arise and be baptized, and wash away your sins, calling on the name of the Lord" (Acts 22:16). Later, St. Paul would describe baptism as "The washing of regeneration and renewing of the Holy Spirit" (Titus 3:5). St. Peter, speaking about how the family of Noah was saved by the Ark, goes on to affirm that "There is also an antitype which now saves us – baptism" (1 Pet. 3:21). These passages had never made sense to me before. But now I understood that these passages clearly teach that baptism is a necessary first step for salvation and that it really is, as the Nicene Creed says, "for the remission of sins." And as is true with the Eucharist, there is no historical evidence that the early Church believed baptism to be purely symbolic.

My discoveries about the hierarchical structure, the liturgical worship, and the sacramental theology of the earliest Christians left me reeling. But then I discovered something else that hit me like a tidal wave: the early Church's view of Scripture and Tradition.

The Early Church Did Not Believe in *Sola Scriptura*

One of the most important tenets held by nearly all Protestants is that of *Sola Scriptura*, that is, the idea that the only completely trustworthy source of spiritual authority is the Bible. Most evangelicals hold that extra-biblical traditions are at best suspect and at worst sent by the devil to confuse Christians and to corrupt the Church. Furthermore, they assert that the Church's increasing reliance on extra-biblical tradition has caused it to grow ever more corrupt through the centuries. In the view of the Protestant reformers, especially the Anabaptists, the way to restore purity to the Church was to jettison tradition and to model church life and theology on the clear teaching of Scripture, even though few could agree on the exact nature of that teaching.

In my mind, a firm adherence to *Sola Scriptura* was non-negotiable. But in *Becoming Orthodox*, I found a good summary of the arguments against this bedrock of evangelical thought.[9] As a committed Baptist, I had always associated the traditions of the Roman Catholic and Orthodox Churches as equivalent to the traditions of men condemned by Jesus (see, for example, Matt. 15:3-20 and 23:1-36) and the "philosophy and empty deceit, according to the tradition of men" that St. Paul warned about (Col. 2:8). I had never entertained the possibility that tradition could sometimes be a good thing.

I knew that St. John wrote that Jesus said and did many things that were not recorded in Scripture (John 20:31) and that St. Luke had explicitly stated that the Lord taught the disciples the meaning of the Scriptures (Luke 24:27, 45). Jesus appeared many times to the Apostles, both individually, in small groups, and as a whole; surely, he spent much of that time equipping them with the knowledge they would need to lead the Church in his absence. He also promised to send his Holy Spirit into the world to "guide you into all truth" (John 16:13) and to remind them of the things that He had taught them.

It is clear that the Apostles did not feel the need to write down everything that they had been taught by their Lord. The reason for this is twofold. First, the epistles were occasional letters written to address specific questions and problems that arose in the churches. If a question did not arise, the Apostles normally did not address it in their letters. Second, the Apostles did not feel the need to write everything down. They lived in an age in which few people could read and

---

[9] See the bibliography at the end of this book for further readings on *Sola Scriptura*.

in which most learning was accomplished by memorizing the words of one's teacher.

As we have seen, St. Paul condemned hollow philosophy and traditions of men. But what did he have to say about the unwritten traditions of Jesus and the Apostles? Again, the answer, found in passages of Scripture that I had never really noticed, was surprising. Consider the following writings of St. Paul:

> "Now I praise you, brethren, that you remember me in all things and keep the traditions just as I delivered them to you" (1 Corinthians 11:2).

> "But we command you, brethren, in the name of our Lord Jesus Christ, that you withdraw from every brother who walks disorderly and not according to the tradition which he received from us" (2 Thessalonians 3:6)

> "Therefore, brethren, stand fast and hold to the traditions which you were taught, whether by word or our epistle" (2 Thessalonians 2:15).

I found the third passage to be especially instructive, because it explicitly refers to a tradition not written down in the New Testament epistles. This made it difficult for me to accept the opinion of evangelical biblical commentators, most of whom claim that the tradition that Paul spoke of was all later incorporated into the New Testament.

As had been the case with the other issues I had recently studied, I found that the Christian writers of the post-apostolic Church confirmed the presence of an authoritative oral tradition that was separate from the New Testament, which itself would not even be in its final form until more than three hundred years after the death of Jesus. It is this tradition, which the Orthodox Church calls Holy Tradition, that guided the Apostles' successors in making decisions about how to conduct the Sacraments, what to teach their parishioners, and how to address the many heresies that arose to challenge the Apostolic Church.

I finally had to admit that even though all evangelical Protestants, including me, said that we believed in *Sola Scriptura*, almost no one truly practices it. Very few, if any Christians, base their doctrine and practice solely on the Bible, for two main reasons. First, much of the Bible is difficult to understand and requires careful interpretation. Also, the Bible by itself does not tell us everything we need to know in order to carry out the various functions of the Church. When I needed to understand the meaning of a particular Scripture passage that was not obvious, what did I do? I read one or more commentaries that gave what the author believed was the most likely interpretation of the passage. But from where did the authors of the commentaries obtain their opinions? The answer was obvious: from one or more earlier commentators. And those scholars, in turn, had learned their interpretations from still earlier commentators. And so on and so on…

I accepted the fact that there existed a large number of traditions of Scripture interpretation: the Baptist tradition, the Methodist tradition, the Anglican tradition, and hundreds of others. And often these traditions contradicted each other. Which one was right? I needed a tie breaker. And then it hit me that the tradition that was most likely to be correct had to be the earliest one – the Orthodox Tradition.

After reading *Becoming Orthodox*, I was convinced of the truth of the Orthodox position on the four major issues discussed in this chapter. But I still had many other questions that required solid answers. So, I called Melanie and asked her if she had any other books on Orthodoxy. Sure enough, she did!

Chapter Eight: Infant Baptism

For as many of you as were baptized
into Christ have put on Christ.
—GALATIANS 3:27

Let the little children come to Me, and do not forbid them; for of
such is the kingdom of God.
—MARK 10:14

Melanie and Bob had one other book similar to *Becoming Orthodox*. The book was *Common Ground*, by Fr. Jordan Bajis. I quickly discovered that while reading Fr. Gillquist's book was like nibbling on a tasty hors d'oeuvre, reading Fr. Jordan's book was like consuming a hearty meal. For while *Becoming Orthodox* is designed to be an introduction to Orthodoxy, with semi-detailed discussions of a few areas where evangelicals and Orthodox disagree, *Common Ground* contains a thorough and detailed discussion of nearly all the key issues. Like Fr. Peter, Fr. Jordan discusses Scripture and Tradition, Church structure and polity, and the Sacraments. His arguments for the Orthodox understanding of these issues reaffirmed what I had read in *Becoming Orthodox*.

Before I picked up *Common Ground*, I had reached a place where I accepted liturgical worship, hierarchical church structure, sacramental worship (to some degree, anyway), and the value of Tradition as both a means of interpreting Scripture and as a guideline for church practice. In reading *Common Ground*, I was now confronted with a convincing argument in favor of something that had previously been anathema to me: infant baptism. Like all Southern Baptists, I was not at all open to the idea of baptizing infants. I thought such a practice to be an unbiblical innovation that had crept into the Church gradually over several hundred years along with all the other "corruptions." Surely the Apostles never baptized anyone who was too young to make a conscious decision to follow Jesus!

Fr. Jordan opened my eyes to a number of Bible passages that seemed to indicate that, in fact, the Apostles did baptize people of all ages. Although I had read these passages dozens of times, my prior commitment to Baptist beliefs had prevented me from seeing them for what they really say.

Biblical and Patristic Support

In the second chapter of Acts, St. Peter preaches to a large crowd of Jews who had come to Jerusalem from all over the Mediterranean world to celebrate the Feast of Weeks, also called Pentecost. After Peter's sermon, his hearers were "cut to the heart" (v. 37) and were persuaded that Jesus was the promised Messiah. We then read that "those who gladly received his word were baptized, and that day about three thousand souls were added to them" (v. 41). Verse 41 does not explicitly tell us that any infants or young children were baptized, but it also does not say that *only* adults were baptized. When Jews went on pilgrimage, they normally took their families with them. Therefore, it is unlikely that only adults were in the crowd that heard St. Peter preach. And like most ancient peoples (and indeed like people in many parts of the world today), the Jews made major religious decisions as a family rather than as individuals. So, if the head of a family were to be baptized, certainly his wife and all his children would too, especially since St. Peter said, "let *every one of you* be baptized for the forgiveness of your sins" (v. 38, emphasis added).

Further evidence for the apostolic practice of infant baptism can be found throughout the book of Acts. In Chapter 11, St. Peter relates Cornelius' meeting an angel, who told him to "Send men to Joppa, and call for Simon whose surname is Peter, who will tell you words by which you and all your household will be saved" (Acts 11:13-14). After Peter arrived, "he commanded them to be baptized in the name of the Lord" (10:48). The clear implication is that the whole household was baptized.

Later, when St. Paul was evangelizing in Philippi, his first convert was a woman named Lydia. Soon after her conversion, "she and her household were baptized" (Acts 16:15). Then, a few days later, after Paul's dramatic deliverance from prison, his jailer also believed in the Lord Jesus. Shortly afterward, we read that "he and all his family were baptized" (Acts 16:33). Finally, in his First Epistle to the Corinthians, St. Paul himself mentions another time that he baptized an entire household, stating simply: "Now I did baptize the household of Stephanus" (1 Cor. 1:16).

The Greek word translated into English as "household" is *oikos*, and as Fr. Jordan points out, "There is no evidence of 'household' being used in either secular Greek, biblical Greek, or in the writings of Hellenistic Judaism which would in any way limit its meaning to adults alone."[10] Moreover, as he adds,

> The Old Testament Hebrew equivalent of this word (*bayit*) always refers to the entire family (even inclusive of up to four generations). The Greek translation of the original Hebrew manuscripts (completed in 250 B.C.), uses *oikos* to translate this Hebrew word as meaning a complete family (men, women, children, adults). The phrase 'he and his house' in the Old Testament particularly refers to the total family, not just to all its adult members.[11]

So, as I was forced to admit, the Apostles did not deny baptism to infants and children, but baptized entire households at a time. But what about the Apostles' immediate successors? Were these biblical examples merely anomalies, or did the Church continue the practice of baptizing people of all ages? Again, Fr. Jordan provided several illuminating statements by the early Church Fathers, including St. Polycarp, St. Justin, and St. Ignatius. But the clearest evidence that infant baptism was

---

[10] Jordan Bajis, *Common Ground: An Introduction to Eastern Christianity for the Western Christian* (Minneapolis: Light and Life Publishing, 1989), 288.

[11] Bajis, *Common Ground*, 288-89 (emphasis in original).

practiced by the early Church comes from the pen of St. Hippolytus of Rome. In his classic manual of Church order *The Apostolic Tradition*, written around the year 215, Hippolytus tells the churches to "Baptize first the children, and if they can speak for themselves, let them do so. Otherwise, let their parents or other relatives speak for them."[12] Finally, a synod held in Carthage in 256 and presided over by St. Cyprian confirmed that baptism of infants was proper and could be done on the third day after the infant was born and did not need to be postponed until the eighth day.

So on yet another issue, I was confronted with clear evidence that the early Church's practice differed from that of my own tradition. I was further challenged when I came to understand the meaning that the early Church attached to baptism.

The Meaning of Baptism

Prior to reading *Common Ground*, I had believed that baptism was "an act of obedience symbolizing the believer's faith in a crucified, buried, and risen Saviour, the believer's death to sin, the burial of the old life, and the resurrection to walk in newness of life in Christ Jesus."[13] In other words, I had seen baptism as merely an event in an individual believer's life, with little impact on the community, except to add another member. But this individualistic mindset would have been completely foreign to the early Church, who viewed a person's baptism as a corporate event, an entrance into the people of God.

Like most Evangelicals who consider themselves part of a "New Testament church," I had based my theology and my ideas about church practice overwhelmingly on the New Testament, resorting to the Old Testament only when necessary. A natural outcome of this mindset was my belief that there is a major break between the Old Covenant and the

[12] Quoted in Bajis, 293.
[13] *The Baptist Faith and Message*, Article 7.

New. But I was beginning to realize that the early Church did not see things that way. As I have mentioned before, the earliest Christians were Jews who believed that the Messiah had come. They saw themselves as the new Israel (cf. Gal. 6:16), and they did not dispense with all of the customs that their forefathers had practiced. To be sure, the early Church did rule that the entire Law of Moses was not binding on Christians (Acts 15). Still, some practices that God had given to the Jews seemed too important to discard. In a few instances, the *form* of practice was modified while the *meaning* of the practice remained the same. A primary example of this is baptism.

In the Old Covenant period, God gave the people of Israel circumcision as a sign of their entrance into the covenant and the people of God. Circumcision was normally performed on the eight day after a child's birth. In the new Covenant period, baptism took the place of circumcision, which the Apostles ruled was no longer necessary. St. Paul provides evidence for this view of baptism in his epistle to the Colossians: "In Him you were also circumcised with the circumcision made without hands...by the circumcision of Christ, buried with him in baptism" (Col. 2:12). St. Justin confirms this idea when he writes "And we, who have approached God through Him, have received not a carnal, but spiritual circumcision...and we have received it through baptism."[14] To be sure, baptism does not guarantee salvation; it only begins the process. But among other things, baptism provides a sign that a person is now part of the new Israel, just as circumcision showed that a person was part of the old Israel. And if an infant was not too young to become a part of God's Old Covenant people, why would anyone be too young to be joined to the Church, God's New Covenant people?

Another meaning that the early Church associated with baptism was that of union with Christ. St. Paul told the Galatians that "as many of you as were baptized into Christ have put on Christ" (3:27). In baptism, Paul writes, a believer is

---

[14] Quoted in Bajis, 292.

"buried with Him through baptism into death" (Rom. 6:4), and "raised with him" (Col. 2:12). A person who is baptized becomes spiritually united with Christ in a real and mystical way that transcends mere symbolism. This union with Christ bestows spiritual benefits to those so united with Him. Whereas the Roman Catholic Church baptizes infants to remove the curse of Original Sin (a concept that developed under the influence of Augustine and that is foreign to the Orthodox Church), the Orthodox Church has always baptized them to bring about a positive blessing. In Fr. Jordan's words, "The child is baptized because [early Eastern Christians] believed that the fruits of this union – power over sin, death, and the devil – could be realized from his earliest days."[15]

In summary, the early Church saw Christianity in a corporate rather than an individual sense. Becoming a Christian was more than simply having one's own soul saved. The first Christians saw conversion to the Christian faith as entering the New Covenant people of God, the New Israel, which is the Body of Christ. And baptism, in addition to washing away a person's sins, resulted in that person being spiritually united with Christ and His Church. Baptism was performed on adult converts and on infants alike. This was the practice of the Church in both East and West, without exception, for the first 1500 years of the Church's history. Then in the early part of the sixteenth century, among one group of the Protestant reformers, it was replaced by a practice that would become one of the hallmarks of evangelical theology: adult-only, or "believers'" baptism.

"Believers' Baptism"

Once while I was in seminary, I watched a movie called *The Radicals*, which chronicles the beginning of the Anabaptist movement. The Anabaptists, the most significant of the radical Protestant Reformers, began the practice of "believers'" baptism, which is still carried on in Southern

---

[15] Bajis, 284.

Baptist and nearly all other evangelical churches. The Anabaptists felt that Luther, Calvin, and Zwingli did not go far enough in dispensing with traditional Church practices. They especially objected to infant baptism. Their interpretation of Scripture convinced them that baptism should only be administered to a person who is fully capable of making a conscious decision to follow Christ. Therefore, in their thinking, baptism must be limited to adults. The truth of this way of thinking seemed as obvious to me as my own existence. While watching *The Radicals*, I remember cheering silently while the early Anabaptist leader Conrad Grebel baptized himself and then George Blaurock, who in turn baptized about fifteen others, giving birth to the Anabaptist movement. I never questioned the rationale behind believers' baptism. But Fr. Jordan opened my eyes to many problems with the idea.

Believers' baptism rests on the idea that in order to be baptized, one must be old enough to make a conscious decision to place one's faith in Christ. This, in turn, implies that faith is primarily a rationalistic idea; that is, it is first and foremost assenting to a set of rational concepts, including that one is a sinner deserving of hell, that one needs Christ as Lord and Savior to be saved, and that one should be baptized in obedience to Christ's command.

But the Greek word *pistis*, which is usually translated as "faith," also includes the ideas of trust and confidence. As Fr. Jordan writes,

> [*Pistis* expresses a relationship of trust. As faith in another human is a bond of trust and love (not primarily a product of analytical reasoning), so is one's faith in God. Therefore, one's ability to use his mind and faculties is not the requirement of faith. The orientation of one's heart and trust is the requirement. It is only this latter sense of faith − as trust − that the Scriptures illustrate.[16]

---

[16] Ibid, 263.

All human beings, even infants, are capable of having a relationship of trust with others. And very young children, while not able to understand as much about God and about faith as an adult, can nevertheless love and trust Him from an early age. Jesus affirmed this when he took up a young child in his arms and referred to "one of these little ones who believe in me" (Matt. 18:6).

Fr. Jordan points out a very serious contradiction that is present in the thinking of Evangelicals and others that deny baptism to infants and small children. Most of these believers treat their children as if they were saved; that is, as if they were Christians. This is because these children are too young to be conscious of their sin, as they have not yet reached the age at which God holds them accountable for their sins (see next section). And yet, this same Evangelical would deny that an unbaptized person is likely to be a true Christian. They would assert that such a person is willfully choosing to disobey a clear commandment of Christ, and therefore has not really accepted Him as Lord. In this is the contradiction – they treat their children as Christians, and yet deny that they can be Christians, because they are not baptized. To be consistent, it would be necessary to either deny that children are in any way Christians or to go ahead and publicly proclaim that these children are indeed Christ's by baptizing them. The latter course is what all Christians did without exception until the Anabaptists appeared.

The Age of Accountability

A final barrier to my accepting the practice of infant baptism was my long-time adherence to the Baptist doctrine of the "age of accountability," the age at which a child supposedly becomes conscious of his sinfulness and the consequences of that sin. Historically, the Anabaptists and their later English followers (known simply as "Baptists") had set different minimum ages for baptism, including twenty, fifteen, and twelve. More recently, Baptists and other evangelicals have decided that rather than setting a uniform age below which no one can be baptized, each child should be interviewed individually to see if he or she is ready.[17] This practice had always seemed completely proper to me. But after reading *Common Ground*, I realized that the age of accountability doctrine was untenable for three reasons.

First, the age of accountability doctrine is unscriptural. Deep down, I had always known this, but I had been afraid to admit it, either to myself or to others. Nowhere in the Bible do we read that a person of any age is too young to be a true believer in Christ, or to be baptized, or to receive Communion. In fact, Jesus seems to have taught just the opposite. Once when some children tried to come to Him, His disciples tried to stop them. As St. Mark tells us, however, "...when Jesus saw it, He was greatly displeased and said to them, 'Let the little children come to Me, and do not forbid them; for of such is the kingdom of God'" (Mark 10:14). Granted, Jesus is not speaking of baptism here, but the principle taught here was understood to apply to baptism, Church membership, and receiving Communion.

Rather than being based on specific biblical teaching, the age of accountability concept is grounded in reason and logic. Surprisingly enough, the source of this doctrine lies not in the Reformation, but within medieval Roman Catholicism. Around the turn of the first millennium, theologians began to prohibit small children from receiving the Eucharist because they were too young to understand what they were doing. Because of this, a child was in serious danger of "eat[ing] and drink[ing] in an unworthy manner" and "eat[ing] and drink[ing] judgment to himself, not discerning the Lord's body" (1 Cor. 11:29). So, while the Eastern Church continued to both baptize and to give Communion to people of all ages, the Church in the West began to give Communion only to older children and adults. Denying Holy Communion to small children provided a

---

[17] Interestingly, the age at which children are being allowed to be baptized in Baptist churches has been steadily decreasing in the last twenty or so years. I have heard many sermons in which pastors have lamented that "Kids are getting baptized too young! Why we're practically baptizing infants!"

logical antecedent to denying them baptism as well. As Fr. Jordan observes, "If the Roman Church were justified in limiting reception of the Lord's Supper until one could understand what he was receiving, how could the Anabaptists be criticized for using the same logic as a rationale for excluding children from baptism?"[18]

A second flaw in the age of accountability doctrine is that it wrongly ties faith to an age limit. As we have seen earlier, the biblical concept of faith is more akin to childlike trust (cf. Matt. 18:3) than it is to mature, rational thought. And the ability and willingness to trust God is not necessarily greater in adults than it is in children. Who has not seen small children who have an obvious trust in, and love for, the Lord Jesus? The history of the Church is full of instances where children willingly gave their lives rather than deny Christ. Moreover, it is impossible to determine precisely when someone is actually cognizant of their need for salvation from sin. As Evangelicals everywhere will affirm, deciding whether a child is ready for baptism is a very difficult thing to do, at least if one wishes to remain faithful to the age of accountability doctrine. And if being older truly makes one's faith more mature and complete, why not wait until someone is twenty or thirty years of age? By these ages, they will have had more time to study the Scriptures and come to understand God's plan of salvation. In reality, none of us will ever fully understand this deep mystery. Given this, why deny baptism to anyone based upon age?

Finally, the age of accountability doctrine is not a protection against spiritual compromise, nor does it insure a pure church. Proponents of the age of accountability doctrine argue that baptizing infants and young children often results in a church later having many adult members that are not true believers in Christ. Many of these fall away, or rather, never really become saved, and pollute the church. But as Fr. Jordan responds, delaying baptism until a child seems to be able to understand what they are doing does not completely solve this

---

[18] Ibid, 269.

problem. A twelve- or fifteen-year-old who makes a profession of faith in Christ and is baptized can just as easily renounce his faith as someone who is baptized as an infant. The Church has always been, and always will be, composed of both "wheat" and "chaff" (see Matt. 13:24-20), and restricting baptism to those supposedly old enough to understand the Gospel is no guarantee of minimizing the "chaff."

One thing that can be done, and that is generally done in the Orthodox Church, to help address this problem is to baptize young children only in families that are active, practicing Christians and who are dedicated to raising the child in the faith. Fr. Jordan well states the problem and its solution:

> When a child of an unbelieving family is baptized, the sacrament is blatantly derided, and its meaning mocked. This, however, should not blind us to the fact that adult baptism *can just as easily be abused*. If an adult is baptized in Christ's name and then later lives a life in contradiction to discipleship, has he not blasphemed the significance of baptism just as much as the unbelieving family's baptism of their child?...The solution to this problem has nothing to do with setting an age requirement for baptism. *The answer lies in the Church living up to its call as the body of Christ* (emphasis in original).[19]

After reading all this, I could no longer deny that infant baptism was scriptural, historical, and logical. Believers' baptism and the doctrine of the age of accountability, however, seemed to be none of these.

So one by one, the many of the doctrines that I had believed since I first began to follow Jesus, including *Sola Scriptura*, *Sola Fide*, non-sacramental theology, and now even believers' baptism, had lost their hold on me. That evening, I said to Jennifer, "You know what? I think that we might be in the wrong church!" I had expected Jennifer to say that I was

---

[19] Ibid, 271.

crazy; the average Baptist missionary wife almost certainly would have. But Jennifer is not your average wife. Like the Old Testament figure of Ruth, who told her mother-in-law Naomi, "Wherever you go, I will go; And wherever you lodge, I will lodge; Your people shall be my people, And your God, my God" (Ruth 1:16), my wonderful and devoted wife looked me straight in the eyes and said, "James, even if you decide to become an Orthodox priest, I am with you." When she said this, I was both delighted and reassured. I now knew that I could pursue this path that might lead to another church without fear of losing my wife and my family.

Chapter Nine: Heaven or Earth?

We knew not whether we were in heaven or on earth, for surely there is no such splendour or beauty anywhere on earth. We cannot describe it to you; only this we know, that God dwells there among humans, and that their service surpasses the worship of all other places. For we cannot forget that beauty.
— ENVOYS OF PRINCE VLADIMIR OF KIEV, AFTER ATTENDING THE DIVINE LITURGY IN HAGIA SOPHIA CATHEDRAL, CONSTANTINOPLE, LATE TENTH CENTURY.[20]

The Church of the Holy Trinity

Shortly after we returned to Banja Luka, Jennifer and I learned that we would soon be hosting two volunteer groups from the United States. The volunteers' primary activities would include observing the work we were doing, offering suggestions for future ministry opportunities, and praying for our work. Both groups would be with us for an entire week, and so I wanted them to receive a good overview of both the town and the life and culture of the people there. Part of the "education" that I had planned for them was visiting the Divine Liturgy at one of the local Orthodox parishes.

Before the groups arrived, I decided to check out a Liturgy myself, so that I might be better prepared to explain what was going on, and to make sure that I was aware of any protocols or rules of etiquette that might exist. In short, I wanted the groups to be able to blend in as well as possible. So, on the Sunday before the first group was to arrive, I headed for the Church of the Holy Trinity, the largest parish in town at that time.

I was totally unprepared for what I saw. It just so happened that the Sunday that I chose to attend was a triple

---

[20] Quoted in Bishop Kallistos Ware, *The Orthodox Church,* fourth ed. (London: Penguin Books, 1997), 264.

celebration. The parish was celebrating two thousand years of Christianity, one thousand years of Christianity among the Serbs, and one hundred years of the Banja Luka archdiocese. As I entered the church grounds, I noticed a large crowd gathered outside, waiting for I knew not what. There were several television cameras and large video screens for the overflow crowd that was expected.

Soon, there came a procession, the likes of which I had never seen, and which I have not seen since. The procession contained several bishops, dozens of priests and deacons, and countless altar boys bearing crosses, candles, fans, icons, and banners. They were singing loudly, triumphantly, and beautifully. They marched into the church, and I and the few hundred others waiting outside followed them in.

And then the Liturgy began. Sweet-smelling smoke filled the room. Icons covered every square inch of the walls and ceilings, reminding me of the great cloud of witnesses that worship with us in heaven (Hebrews 12:1). A beautiful choir gave me the sense that the room was filled with angels. The pomp and solemnity, together with the non-stop prayers and expressions of worship, reminded me of the scenes of heavenly worship described in the Bible. In short, I was stunned. Like the Kievian envoys a thousand years before me, I did not know whether I was in heaven or on earth!

The richness of the Divine Liturgy contrasted greatly with the dryness of the Baptist service in Banja Luka, with its few short prayers, its generally superficial songs (when there *were* songs!), its interminable sermons, and its four bare walls. When I left the Liturgy, I thought "Wow, now *that* is worship!"

After I had visited the Divine Liturgy twice, I shared my excitement about it to Bob. I said, "You absolutely *must* attend a Liturgy! It will blow you away!" I told him about the richness of the worship, including the music, the icons, the incense, and the general majesty and God-centeredness. I said, "Now *this* is how we ought to worship!" He was not overly impressed. He said, "That is certainly a valid way to worship, but it is very much conditioned by the culture of the first few centuries. Cultures change, and worship should be able to adapt itself to changing cultures and societies." I felt that he certainly had a good point. His statement prompted me to seek an answer to another question: Is the worship style of the Orthodox Church just one valid style among many, or is it the way that we *ought* to worship?

The Worship of Heaven

Again, Becoming Orthodox helped to answer this question. As Fr. Peter points out, the people of ancient Israel were not free to worship in any way that they pleased. Rather, the worship of Israel followed a specific pattern commanded by God himself, a pattern that was modeled after the worship that continually occurs in heaven (see Hebrews 8:5 and 9:23). Since the Church is the new Israel, it naturally follows that the early Church would have likewise attempted to follow the heavenly pattern of worship as closely as possible. But what is worship in heaven like?

Obviously, no one this side of paradise can fully grasp the nature of the worship that continually occurs in the presence of the Lord. Still, Scripture gives us two important glimpses of the heavenly adoration of God. One such description is the Apostle John's vision of the throne of God found in the fourth chapter of the book of Revelation. In that passage, John sees the Son of God sitting on a throne, surrounded by twenty-four elders dressed in white robes. Before the throne burn seven lamps of fire. The elders continually prostrate themselves before the Lord, while flying creatures sing "Holy, holy, holy, Lord God Almighty, who was and is to come" (Rev. 4:8). Clearly, this nonstop worship of the Lord Jesus would have been a sight to see!

A second passage that gives us a glimpse into heavenly worship is found in the sixth chapter of Isaiah. In this chapter, Isaiah relates his call to be God's prophet. I had long been familiar with this passage, but like most of my evangelical friends and colleagues, I had studied it primarily for its narration of a "call to missions" experience, rather than for what it had to say about worship. The text of Isaiah's call is well known, but the first part bears repeating:

> In the year that King Uzziah died, I saw the Lord sitting on a throne, high and lifted up, and the train of His robe filled the temple. Above it stood seraphim; each one had six wings: with two he covered his face, with two he covered his feet, and with two he flew. And one cried to another and said:
>
> "Holy, holy, holy is the LORD of hosts;
> The whole earth is full of His glory!"
> And the posts of the door were shaken by the voice of him who cried out, and the house was filled with smoke. So I said:
>
> "Woe is me, for I am undone!
> Because I am a man of unclean lips,
> And I dwell in the midst of a people of unclean lips;
> For my eyes have seen the King,
> The LORD of hosts."
>
> Then one of the seraphim flew to me, having in his hand a live coal which he had taken with the tongs from the altar. And he touched my mouth with it, and said:
>
> "Behold, this has touched your lips;
> Your iniquity is taken away,
> And your sin purged" (Isaiah 6:1-7).

As Fr. Peter points out, the worship that is revealed in this passage is multi-sensory. We see worship first of all as *seeing*: there is the Lord on a throne, high and lifted up, with the train of his robe filling the temple. We also notice seraphim flying around the altar, continually singing praises to God. We also see worship as *hearing*, as we hear the song "Holy, holy, holy" being sung in a loud voice. We encounter worship as *taste* and *touch*, as one of the seraphim touches Isaiah's lips with the coal, a gesture signifying forgiveness and cleansing. Finally, the worship in heaven includes an element of *smell*, in that the house is filled with smoke.

After reading this passage with a fresh perspective, I saw that the worship that continually occurs in heaven is far different from that which is conducted in the overwhelming majority of evangelical churches. Isaiah 6 and Revelation 4 helped me to understand that the Orthodox Church's practice of decorating its church buildings with images, using incense, wearing vestments, encouraging prostrations, singing liturgical hymns like the Trisagion ("Holy, Holy, Holy"), and even the practice of placing Holy Communion directly into the worshippers' mouths reflects the multi-sensory worship spoken of in Scripture. I also began to understand that when we worship God, we are not doing so on our own; rather, we are merely joining in the unceasing worship that occurs at the very throne of God. As Fr. Peter writes,

> Truth is, there is just one Divine Liturgy, one Holy Communion, in all the universe – the one in heaven. We who gather as the Church here on earth are called to join in and participate with heaven's hosts. And to do so, we take great pains in our worship to make it consistent – and not to clash –with the worship before the throne of God. Or, to use the words of the Lord's Prayer, we want to be sure that in our worship we are carrying out God's will "on earth as it is in heaven."[21]

Having read Fr. Peter's explanation of Orthodox worship and having personally experienced the beauty and majesty of the Divine Liturgy several times, I was now a true believer in the Orthodox style of worship. So when the volunteer groups were in town, I was excited to be able to give them a taste of the Divine Liturgy. As a result of my reading

---

[21] Fr. Peter Gillquist, *Becoming Orthodox: A Journey to the Ancient Christian Faith*, 2nd ed. (Ben Lomond, CA: Conciliar Press, 1992), 83.

and my previous visits to the service, I was able to explain some of the features of the church building and the service itself. By the time the second group arrived, I found myself actually defending the Church against their Protestant objections. I also found myself crossing myself and making *metanias* (partial prostrations) along with the other worshippers. Some members of that second group seemed to think that I might have lost my mind! There was definitely a change taking place in my thinking about the practice of worship.

After I had attended the Divine Liturgy with the first group of volunteers. I asked them, "So, what did you think of it?" All of them politely expressed generally positive sentiments. However, one of the men, said "I didn't like the fact that there was a gigantic icon of Mary above the altar. It was even bigger than any of the icons of Jesus! Why does the Orthodox Church give so much attention to Mary?" I found myself unable to give him a satisfactory answer. A little later I asked myself, "Why indeed *does* the Church exalt Mary so?"

Mary

Once again, Fr. Peter came to my rescue. Like me, he had once struggled with the Church's veneration of Mary. As committed evangelicals, both Fr. Peter and I had reacted against anything that seemed "too Catholic." And nothing seemed more "Catholic" than venerating Mary! As Fr. Peter points out, however, veneration of Mary is both biblical and rooted in history. It is warranted first of all because Mary is a model of obedience for all Christians. When the Archangel Gabriel appeared to Mary and revealed God's plan for her, her response was simply, "Let it be to me according to your word" (Luke 1:38). God did not force his will upon Mary. She could have said "no." But in saying "yes," she set an example for all believers in Christ. In fact, she can truly be called the first person to receive Christ. And as a result of her obedience, the Savior of our souls came into the world.

Both Gabriel and Mary's cousin Elizabeth recognized that Mary was special when they told her, "Blessed are you among women!" (Luke 1:28, 42). Moreover, upon hearing these words, Mary prophesied "henceforth all generations will call me blessed" (Luke 1:48). So, in honoring Mary, the Church is simply acknowledging the truth of the words of these great servants of God. In Fr. Peter's words, "Essentially, all generations in Church history have [called Mary blessed]; only those of the last few centuries have faltered."[22] For many Evangelicals, however, this exaltation of Mary is interpreted as worship of her, placing her on the same level as Christ himself. If this were true, it would certainly be tantamount to idolatry. But nothing could be farther from the truth. While Christians *venerate* (i.e. pay respect to) Mary, they reserve true *worship* to God alone.

After the volunteers had gone, I continued to attend the Divine Liturgy, going nearly every Sunday. When possible, I took Jennifer with me. I would attend the Liturgy in the morning and the Baptist service in the afternoon. Whereas my attendance at the Baptist service was done totally out of obligation, my participation in the Divine Liturgy was done out of pure joy. After I had attended the Liturgy several times, I decided to try to speak to one of the priests. However, I felt a little self-conscious and afraid to do so, largely because of my job, and so unfortunately, I never did. Still, through the Liturgy alone, the Serbs were beginning to convert me!

---

[22] Gillquist, 108.

Chapter Ten: Crisis

It is hard for you to kick against the goads.
—ACTS 26:14

Changes

By the first of December, I had attended the Divine Liturgy several times and had read and reread *Becoming Orthodox, Common Ground,* and *The Orthodox Church.* By then Jennifer had also read the books and like me, she had found them persuasive. As a result of our reading and our visits to the Liturgy, Jennifer and I now found ourselves in a theological crisis. When we had arrived in Banja Luka, we were confident that our Baptist theology and practice were solidly based on the Bible and Church history. We were certain that the Baptist church, along with most other evangelical churches, was a "New Testament Church," meaning that it was a faithful reproduction of the church of the Apostles.

As late as early October 2000, we were convinced that the first-century Church was non-sacramental. In other words, Peter and Paul and the others saw baptism and the Eucharist as being purely symbolic rituals that do not impart any kind of supernatural grace. We believed that early Christian worship was unstructured and centered on preaching; it certainly was not liturgical! We also held that the polity of the apostolic Church was more or less congregational, without any semblance of "monarchical" bishops. We were certain that all these beliefs were clearly taught by the Bible. But after reading just three books, we were no longer sure if any of our positions on these issues were correct. Through our reading, we had been presented solid biblical and historical evidence that the Church was in fact sacramental in theology, liturgical in worship practice, and hierarchical in structure from its very beginning.

Before we began studying Orthodoxy, we held firmly to the twin Protestant pillars of *Sola Scriptura* (the Bible alone is a valid source of authority; extra-biblical traditions are untrustworthy) and *Sola Fide* (salvation comes through faith alone; works play no role whatsoever). Moreover, the Southern Baptist core doctrines of "believers'" (not infant!) baptism and the eternal security of the believer (salvation can never be forfeited once obtained) were deeply ingrained in our thinking. Moreover, practices such as praying to saints, praying for the departed, and venerating icons were anathema to us!

But by December our thinking had changed, and we were not completely sure what we believed. On some issues, such as the nature of the early Church and infant baptism, we were almost completely convinced of the Orthodox position. But we were not fully sold on the Orthodox view of salvation or on the validity of venerating saints and praying for the departed. Clearly, we needed to do some more study!

Outside Help

Since more study would not be possible until we could get our hands on more books, I decided to try and contact one of the former Campus Crusade for Christ workers who had converted to Orthodoxy along with Fr. Peter Gillquist. I managed to find the e-mail address of Fr. Gordon Walker, the founding pastor of St. Ignatius' Antiochian Orthodox Church in Franklin, Tennessee. Since Fr. Gordon had once been a Southern Baptist pastor and had attended the same seminary as me, I figured that he might best be able to relate to my struggle and to answer my questions. Fr. Gordon answered my first e-mail very quickly. Then, over the next several weeks, he very graciously and patiently answered my questions about Orthodoxy. Fr. Gordon helped me find answers to many of the questions about Orthodoxy that had nagged me. Most importantly, he advised Jennifer and me to take our time and make sure that converting to Orthodoxy was really something that we wanted to do. Fr. Gordon was a great help to us, and our e-mail correspondence forged a friendship that has lasted to this day.

I still had a great deal of reading that I wanted to do, but I had no way to get hold of the books I needed to read. Providentially, Jennifer and I had previously scheduled a trip to the States that would last from mid-December to mid-January. So, I logged onto the internet and began ordering books, which I had sent to our parents' homes, where I would soon be able to read them. In all, I ordered about a dozen books. I had so many burning questions that I had to have answered. Would the other books be able to answer them to my satisfaction?

I would soon find out.

Chapter Eleven: More Reading

Show me Your ways, O LORD;
Teach me Your paths.
Lead me in Your truth and teach me,
You are the God of my salvation;
On You I wait all the day.
—PSALM 25:4-5

Father Paul and Saint Paul

As soon as we reached my parents' house in the northern suburbs of Houston, I tore into the packages that were waiting for me and began voraciously reading the books that they contained. In the four weeks that we spent with our parents, I spent every spare minute eagerly seeking the answers to the remaining questions that I had about Orthodoxy. Of course, some of the dozen or so books proved to be more helpful than others. One book that I found especially helpful was *An Eastern Orthodox Response to Evangelical Claims*, by Fr. Paul O'Callaghan. In this work, Fr. Paul lists common objections and questions to Orthodox distinctives and then convincingly answers them. Many of the questions listed were the exact things for which I needed clarification. Through his book, Fr. Paul helped me overcome many of my doubts about Orthodoxy.

A second critical book that I read was *The Orthodox Study Bible* (OSB), which at the time consisted of the New King James translation of the New Testament with commentary and study aids written by Orthodox scholars.[23] I had wondered how the Orthodox Church interpreted the numerous passages that I thought firmly supported *Sola Fide*. In his epistles to the Romans and the Galatians, St. Paul repeatedly affirms that salvation does not come as a result of keeping the Mosaic Law,

---

[23] As of this writing, the complete *Orthodox Study Bible*, with both the NKJV New Testament and a fresh translation of the Old Testament from the Septuagint, has just been published by Thomas Nelson Publishing.

but by faith.[24] Like all Evangelicals, I assumed that because salvation is by faith, it is by faith *alone*. Of all the New Testament passages that seemed to teach this idea, none seemed to do so as clearly as Ephesians 2:8-9, which I had memorized and quoted hundreds of times. In these verses, St. Paul affirms: "For by grace you have been saved through faith, and that not of yourselves; it is the gift of God, not of works, lest anyone should boast." To me, this was a one-passage proof par excellence that works play no role whatsoever in a person's salvation.

But the OSB helped me to understand for the first time in my life that there was another side to the story. All of a sudden, passages that affirm the necessity of good works for salvation seemed to appear out of nowhere! Consider the following statements of Jesus:

> "...if you want to enter into life, keep the commandments" (Matt. 19:17).

> "...those who have done good [will go] to the resurrection of life, and those who have done evil to the resurrection of condemnation" (John 5:29).

> "Most assuredly, I say to you, if anyone keeps my word, he shall never see death" (John 8:51).

Even in my beloved book of Romans, the book that seemed above all others to teach *Sola Fide*, I read the following words of St. Paul, to my great consternation:

> [God] will render to each according to his deeds, eternal life to those who by patient continuance in doing good seek for glory, honor, and immortality, but to those who are self-seeking and do not obey the truth, but obey unrighteousness—indignation and wrath, tribulation and anguish on every soul of man

---

[24] See, for example, Rom. 3:22, 27, 4:4-5, 11:6 and Gal. 2:16.

who does evil...but glory, honor, and peace to everyone who works what is good... (Rom. 2:6-10)

These and other New Testament passages[25] presented me with a dilemma. Was there a contradiction? Did Jesus and St. Paul disagree on how one is saved? Was St. Paul conflicted, sometimes affirming and sometimes denying that works are necessary for salvation? Finally, St. James helped me find the solution to the problem. For St. James is the only New Testament author to use the phrase "faith alone." We find the important phrase in James 2:24: "You see that a man is justified by works, and *not* by faith alone (*emphasis added*)." This verse, more than any other, had never made sense to me as an evangelical Protestant. My solution had been to ignore it and other such verses that did not fit into the scheme of Baptist theology. Now, I felt that I finally understood this and the other troublesome passages. Taking these verses together with the "no works" passages, I finally understood the New Testament's teaching on the relationship of faith and works, namely, while salvation is not by works alone, neither is it by faith alone. For as St. James affirms earlier, "faith by itself, if it does not have works, is dead" (2:17). In other words, true saving faith and works are inseparable; they are two sides of the same coin. Works are necessary for salvation exactly because faith is necessary for salvation.

The Fathers and *The Way*

A third work that proved invaluable in moving me toward Orthodoxy was *The Apostolic Fathers*, translated by Fr. Jack Sparks. Here I was able to read what Christian leaders of the late first and early second centuries, many of whom had learned their doctrine directly from the Apostles, had to say about the issues on which Evangelicals and Orthodox

---

[25] See, for example, Matt. 7:21 and 25:34-36; John 10:27-28; Acts 10:35; 2 Cor. 5:10; Rev. 20:12. I had certainly never underlined or highlighted any of these verses in my Bible!

Christians disagreed. Now I could put the claims of Frs. Peter Gillquist and Jordan Bajis to the test. In every instance, they passed! I read St. Ignatius of Antioch calling the Eucharist "the medicine of immortality" and urging local Christians to be obedient to their bishops. I heard St. Clement of Rome arguing for apostolic succession and describing a threefold division of Church leadership. I observed how the author of the *Didache* urged the use of liturgical prayer in the Eucharist, baptism by triple immersion, and fasting on Wednesdays and Fridays. Reading these works further confirmed that in both its theology and its liturgical practice, the Orthodox Church more closely resembled the Church of the Apostles than did any other Christian tradition.

By this time, I felt that I almost completely agreed with Orthodoxy. The final nail in the coffin of my allegiance to the Baptist church was my reading of *The Way: What Every Protestant Should Know About the Orthodox Church* by Clark Carlton. This is the most persuasive book for Orthodoxy that I have ever read, but it is not for the easily offended! Evangelicals and other Protestants who read The Way must be ready for some "tough love," because Carlton does not pull any punches in his critique of evangelical theology and praxis. I think that one reason that I connected so well with this book is that the author is, like me, a former Southern Baptist who had attended seminary. In *The Way*, Carlton powerfully argues against Protestant distinctives such as *Sola Scriptura* and *Sola Fide* and argues for Orthodox theology and practice. However, the part of the book that had the greatest impact on me was Carlton's discussion of the Church.

The Church

Never a highly individualistic Christian, I had always had a high view of the Church. I had always loved the biblical metaphors for the Church, especially the Body of Christ, the Bride of Christ, and God's household. Nevertheless, having been influenced by my pastors and seminary professors, I believed that the Church was "an autonomous local congregation of baptized believers, associated by covenant in the faith and fellowship of the gospel,"²⁶ and nothing more.

In all of my studies of the Bible, I had missed several critical passages about the Church, passages that suggest that it is much more than a mere assembly of believers. In his Epistle to the Ephesians, St Paul writes that the Church is "His body, the *fullness of Him* who fills all in all" (1:23; *emphasis added*). I had to reflect for a long time about the meaning of this passage. St. Paul is teaching that as the Body of Christ, the Church is the visible presence of Christ on earth. Indwelt by the Holy Spirit, the Church contains the fullness of God! This is a mystery that we will not be able to fully grasp on this side of heaven: The Church, while distinct from Christ as a person's head is distinct from his body, is nonetheless in a mystical and real union with Christ, as a body is in union with the head.

St. Paul also uses strong language about the Church in his first epistle to Timothy. He counsels Timothy to "conduct yourself [well] in the house of God, which is the church of the living God, the pillar and ground of the truth" (1 Tim. 3:15). In other words, the Church is not only the source ("the ground") of all Christian truth, be it Scripture or Tradition, but it is also the arbiter and interpreter of truth ("the pillar"). In seeing the Church as the source of the truth, I accepted the fact (painful for me at the time) that the Church came before the Bible. This further implies that the Church has the right and the ability to interpret the Scriptures, rather than the Scriptures (or rather, my interpretation of them) judging the Church. But exactly which church is Paul calling the pillar and ground of the truth?

When Jesus ascended into heaven, he did not leave behind any writings or any type of school. He left one thing behind: the Church. And he made several promises about the Church. First, He promised that He would protect the Church when he said "the gates of Hades shall not prevail against it" (Matt. 16:18). Second, he promised that He would be present with the Church: "Lo, I am with you always, even unto the end

---

²⁶ *The Baptist Faith and Message*, Article Six.

of the age" (Matt. 28:20). Finally, he promised that through His Spirit, he would guide the Church when he told the disciples: "He, the Spirit of truth...will guide you into all truth; for he will not speak of His own authority, but whatever He hears he will speak; and He will tell you things to come" (John 16:13).

As a good Baptist, I had always believed that after the last of the Apostles had died, the Church gradually fell into an ever increasing amount of error, adopting more and more beliefs and practices that were contrary to the teaching of Jesus and the Apostles (and, of course, the Baptist church!). But taking these verses literally required that I abandon this assumption. For if this had truly happened, then Jesus had not remained with His Body, the Holy Spirit had not guided the Church into all truth, and indeed, the gates of Hades had prevailed against her. Ironically, like nearly all Evangelicals, I had always believed that the Holy Spirit had guided the early Church to correctly select which books did and did not belong in the New Testament. Would the same Spirit fail to also guide the Church in its statements of doctrine and in its worship?

So again, I had to find an answer to this very important question: To which church was Jesus and St. Paul referring? Was it the Baptist church? Could it have been any of the many Protestant churches? Clearly not, because none of these were founded by Jesus himself. Now certainly, the founders of most of the thousands of Protestant denominations would say that the Lord was leading them to do so. But anyone can say this, and many false teachers do. Would Jesus really lead people to create division in the body for which he prayed, "That they may all be one" (John 17:21)? I could no longer escape the historical fact that the Church that Jesus had founded had never ceased to exist, even though I had not known of her existence for most of my life. The Church has never been perfect, due to the simple fact that it is made up of sinful human beings. But, as Jesus promised, it has persevered despite hundreds of years of persecution by pagans, Muslims, Communists, and other hostile groups. Moreover, as a whole, the Church has not fallen into error or decay. At last I had to admit the truth of something that I had been resisting for several months: the Orthodox Church was not simply the *closest* of all Christian traditions to the New Testament Church. As Carlton writes: "The Orthodox Church does not imitate the Church of the New Testament, She *is* the Church of the New Testament" (emphasis in original).[27]

It finally dawned on me that I was not part of the Body of Christ, the Church that Jesus founded and sent his Spirit to guide, the fullness of Him and the pillar and ground of the truth. I now had a choice: I could continue to pursue the Christian life outside of the Church that Christ founded (hardly an enviable situation) or submit myself to her. I realized that if Christ had truly guided his Church into all truth, then any problems that I had with her doctrine or practices were problems with my thinking and not with the Church. Though I still had many questions, I decided to submit to the Church's wisdom, trusting that in time, my questions would be answered.

After this, I told Jennifer: "It's over. I'm no longer a Baptist!"

---

[27] Clark Carlton, *The Way: What Every Protestant Should Know about the Orthodox Faith* (Salisbury, MA: Regina Orthodox Publishing, 1997), 84.

Chapter Twelve: Intermission, Part Two

We have seen the True Light!
We have received the heavenly Spirit!
Worshipping the undivided Trinity
Who has saved us!
—POST-COMMUNION HYMN,
DIVINE LITURGY OF ST. JOHN CHRYSOSTOM

Worship

Since about the first of December, Jennifer and I had confided in our friends and colleagues Bob and Melanie about our growing affinity for Orthodoxy. They had read the two books that we had borrowed from them, and like us, they had found much of what they read to be quite persuasive. I will never forget something that Bob said after we had spent a couple of hours discussing the points raised in the books. After I said to Bob, "We may well end up going into the Orthodox Church," he looked me in the eyes and said, "Well, we may just go with you." In spite of these words, Jennifer and I could tell that Bob and Melanie were not as enthusiastic as we were. One telltale sign of this was that neither of them visited the Divine Liturgy in Banja Luka or in the States, where they also spent the Christmas holidays in 2000-2001.

One time in December when I had described to Bob how wonderful I thought the Divine Liturgy was, he said to me, "Well, it is great that you love the Divine Liturgy *here*, but if you convert to Orthodoxy, you will eventually have to go home and find a parish in the States to attend. What if the services there are not quite so wonderful? You should make sure that you find the worship in a parish in the States as fulfilling as you have found it to be here!" I thought that he had a good point. What would we discover once we arrived in the States? Would the worship in the States be as magnificent as that which we had seen in Banja Luka? Would we find further confirmation of the truth and beauty of Orthodoxy, or would we find that Orthodoxy was merely a quaint, outdated, mainly Eastern European phenomenon based more on the traditions of men than on the teaching of the early Church?

As soon as we arrived at my parents' house, I searched the internet for the closest Orthodox parish. I quickly found one that was only a few miles from my parents' house – Saint Anthony the Great Antiochian Orthodox Church in Spring, Texas. On our last Sunday before we returned to Bosnia, Jennifer and I attended the Divine Liturgy at St. Anthony's while my parents watched the children. The service was everything that I thought and hoped it would be. Even though there were not nearly as many icons as we had seen in Banja Luka, and the choir was much smaller, the service was still beautiful. And to really sweeten the deal, it was all in English! Our experience at St. Anthony's further confirmed our sense that God was leading us into Orthodoxy.

Our experience at St. Anthony's was in marked contrast to one that we had a couple of weeks earlier. On the first Sunday after we arrived in Houston, we had visited the morning worship service at the Baptist church where we were members, the church in whose missionary house we had stayed two years previously. We had wondered if visiting our home church might put the brakes on our rapid march toward Orthodoxy. Would visiting a larger church with better music and a more experienced preacher than the Banja Luka Baptist Church remind us that we really were Baptists deep down?

Far from it! Whereas previously we had loved our church and its services, now we both felt like fish out of water. All I could think about was how I missed the beauty of the Divine Liturgy. Jennifer and I felt guilty about it, but we could not deny that we just wanted to get out of there and get back home. How refreshing it was two weeks later when we attended the Liturgy at St. Anthony's!

By New Year's Day 2001, after reflecting at length on our reading and our varied worship experiences, and after much prayer, Jennifer and I firmly believed that it was God's will for us to convert to Orthodoxy. But very soon after that day, God upped the ante on me once more. Once again, He used a book to communicate His will to me. Late one night, only a few days before we were to fly back to Bosnia, I was reading the wonderful book *At the Corner of East and Now* by Frederica Mathewes-Green. In one section of her book, Mathewes-Green describes the *proskomedia* (preparation of the bread and wine) service that every priest performs quietly prior to celebrating the Divine Liturgy. I found myself captivated by the beautiful words that the priest recites while cutting out the Lamb (the piece of the loaf that eventually becomes the Body and Blood of Christ), "He was led as a sheep to the slaughter, and as a lamb before its shearer is dumb, so he opened not his mouth. In his humiliation justice was denied him. Who shall describe his generation? For his life is taken up from the earth" (Isaiah 53:7-8, LXX).

As I read these words, I once again felt that still, small, inaudible voice speaking to me, saying, "This is what *you* are going to do." I knew then that not only was I supposed to convert to Orthodoxy, but I was also destined to become a priest! I shared this experience with Jennifer, and as always, she was totally supportive. But now I had another big problem to solve. While on the plane back to Bosnia, I kept asking myself, "How can I become an Orthodox priest while at the same time working as a Baptist missionary?"

Retreat

A couple of days after returning to Europe, Jennifer and I rushed off to Slovenia to attend a spiritual retreat for all of our organization's missionaries in our area. The retreat included a good deal of rest and relaxation, along with daily Bible study sessions led by a pastor from the United States. Of course, Jennifer and I enjoyed the rest and the fellowship with our friends and colleagues. Still, the whole week we were there, we experienced that same "fish out of water" feeling that we had felt when we had visited our home church in the States. This feeling served as still further confirmation that we really did not belong in the Baptist church any more.

During one of the Bible studies, the pastor spoke on St. Peter's sermon in the second chapter of Acts, a passage that I had spent much time studying lately. As he made his way through the passage, I began to wonder how he would handle one particular statement near the end of the chapter. In verse 37, we read that after St. Peter finished his sermon, his listeners "were cut to the heart, and said to Peter and the rest of the apostles, 'Men and brethren, what shall we do?'"

St. Peter's answer, of course, was "'Repent, and let every one of you be baptized in the name of Jesus Christ for the remission of sins; and you shall receive the gift of the Holy Spirit'" *(v. 38)*. I was curious to see what the pastor would say about the five troublesome little words in the middle of the sentence: "for the remission of sins." As we have already seen, this passage is one of many that clearly states that baptism washes away sins, granting us forgiveness. For the first 1500 years of the Church's history, no one questioned the plain meaning of the text. For many of the Protestant reformers, however, this plain meaning did not fit into their theological system, and so they began to either rationalize away the obvious interpretation of the text or to simply ignore the text altogether. In doing so, they set an example that is followed by the overwhelming majority of evangelical Protestants today.

Not surprisingly, the pastor at our retreat spoke at length about repenting, being baptized, and receiving the Holy Spirit. But he totally skipped over the controversial phrase. This convinced me once and for all that I could no longer accept the evangelical hermeneutical system, which too often takes certain parts of Scripture and elevates them above others, making an interpretive grid out of the former while ignoring or rationalizing away the latter. It finally clicked in my mind that the Orthodox interpretation of Scripture was the most consistent one, the one that takes *all* passages seriously, not effectively doing away with those that do not fit into its scheme.

To paraphrase Fr. Peter Gillquist's sentiment given in *Becoming Orthodox*, I was finally beginning to understand all the verses that I had *not* underlined in my Bible!

Chapter Thirteen: Orthodox at Heart

For where your treasure is,
there your heart will be also.
—LUKE 12:34

Undercover

Before we had departed for the States in December, Jennifer and I had agreed with our fellow team members Bob and Melanie to continue to study Orthodoxy and to prayerfully seek God's will on whether or not to continue toward the Ancient Faith. After the retreat was over, the four of us came together to discuss what we had learned. Jennifer and I were somewhat disappointed to learn that while we had moved *toward* Orthodoxy, our dear friends had moved *away* from it. Whereas we were ready to convert as soon as we could, they had too many questions and doubts about Orthodoxy to do so. Many of the answers Jennifer and I had found to the questions that we had all had about the Church did not satisfy Bob and Melanie.

Soon after our meeting, Bob and I had another long conversation, in which I revealed to him that not only did Jennifer and I desire to convert to Orthodoxy, but also that I sensed that God was calling me to become an Orthodox priest. To my surprise, he was not in the least caught off guard. In fact, I think he had been expecting this. He and his family were about to go to Prague for a three week long training conference, and he encouraged me to keep praying and thinking about what to do. I promised I would.

During February, while Bob and Melanie were gone, I continued carrying out my job responsibilities as best I could, given that in my heart I was now fully Orthodox. I began keeping an Orthodox rule of liturgical prayer, I attended the Divine Liturgy as often as I could, and I continued to read the *Orthodox Study Bible* and other books about Orthodoxy. I now felt very torn, as if I were an undercover Orthodox "agent" merely posing as a Baptist missionary.

Part of me felt that Jennifer and I should just go home and begin the formal conversion process immediately. Jennifer tended to agree with this inclination. But then the practical side of me kicked in. Jennifer and I were doing very well financially, being able to save quite a bit of money each month. As had been the case when I was in South Carolina contemplating whether to quit my job and go to seminary, I realized that I had no job to go back to in the States. How would I support myself and my growing family (we were by then expecting a third child) if we left the mission field? Unfortunately, I had almost totally forgotten the lessons that God had taught me eight years earlier about how He provides for all our needs.

So, I decided to be an "undercover" Orthodox Christian while continuing to work indefinitely as a Baptist missionary. This would have been hard enough if I were still a regular missionary, serving with only Bob and Melanie. For example, if and when I led a Serb unbeliever to faith in Christ, what church would I encourage him to join? I knew it could not be the Baptist church! But my "undercover" plan was complicated further by two things: First, I had just been placed in a supervisory role, and second, another missionary family was coming to join our team in March. This couple was to be under my supervision. As Jennifer pointed out to me, I would soon have to carry the Baptist "flag" and lead a team, which would be impossible to do convincingly if I no longer even agreed with much of the Baptist church's teaching.

There was another complication in my plan. We had heard that our organization's board of trustees was seriously considering requiring all of its missionaries to sign a statement saying that they fully agreed with *The Baptist Faith and Message*. Just a few months earlier, Jennifer and I would have gladly signed that statement. But now we knew we could not. One day, we received an e-mail from the board's headquarters with "Baptist Faith and Message" in the subject line. I thought, "Oh great! I guess this is the end of our missionary career!" Fortunately, the message, which had been written by the president of the board, said that despite what rumors we had heard, our missionaries would *not* have to sign the statement. [28] I breathed a sigh of relief. Our "cover" had not been blown!

But it did not matter.

As a new supervisor, I was scheduled to attend the same training conference in March that Bob and Melanie had attended in February. I had absolutely no desire to go, but in keeping with my plan, I resolved to attend anyway. I consoled myself with the thought that at least I could sneak off and attend the Orthodox parish in Prague a few times! The day after Bob and Melanie returned from Prague, Jennifer and I met with Bob. Trying to avoid the subject of us possibly leaving the mission field, I rattled on for nearly an hour about all that Jennifer and I had done to prepare for their arrival of our new team members, and what still needed to be done. Bob patiently waited until I was done, and then he turned to me and abruptly said, "So, have you decided what to do about converting to Orthodoxy?" I was busted!

I told him of my plan to stay in Banja Luka, while Jennifer and I would try to be undercover Orthodox Christians. Boldly and wisely, Bob said, "That's not going to work." He proceeded to explain how at the training conference, I would be asked to share my own vision for the expansion of the Baptist faith in my adopted country and to develop a plan to make it happen. He described how the entire month would be, in his words, "one big pep rally for the Baptist missionary effort." Finally, he said with love and frankness, "If you two are definitely planning to convert to Orthodoxy, then you need to go ahead and go home now." He assured us that he was not trying to get rid of us. But he knew that my "undercover" plan was complete folly. Jennifer fully agreed with him, and between the two of them they persuaded me.

The next day, I went and obtained a partial refund on my plane ticket to Prague. Then I called my supervisor Ted in

---

[28] Interestingly enough, after only a few months, the board of trustees reversed itself and did require all missionaries to sign the statement.

Zagreb. I said, "Ted, I'm not going to Prague, and I need to come up there and talk to you about something."

Resignation

After hanging up the phone, Ted assumed that the reason I had decided not to go on the trip to Prague was simply because I had decided not to serve as a supervisor any more. In this he was correct. However, he was not at all prepared to hear the specific reason *why* I no longer wanted to be a supervisor.

A few days after I called Ted, Jennifer and I drove to Zagreb, Croatia, to meet with Ted and his wife Teresa. After a little bit of uncomfortable small talk, I said, "Ted, I don't want to beat around the bush with you. Jennifer and I have been studying the Orthodox Church, and we have decided to convert to Orthodoxy. Therefore, we will be resigning our positions as missionaries and returning to the States."

Ted was stunned. I don't think he would have been more shocked if I had told him that I had murdered fifty people and was on the run from the Banja Luka police! At first, he didn't know what to say. Finally, he began to try and talk us out of it. He raised objection after objection about Orthodoxy, and I answered them as best I could. All of his objections concerned issues that Jennifer I had grappled with ourselves and had eventually overcome. His greatest problem with Orthodoxy was that the Church does not agree with any of the five points of Calvinism! At one point, he even ran out of the room and brought back a paper that he had written in seminary about the alleged errors of Orthodoxy. Needless to say, I did not find the paper persuasive.

After an hour or so, Ted realized that he was not going to talk us out of becoming Orthodox, so he changed tactics. Now he tried to convince us to stay in spite of the fact that we were Orthodox in heart – the very idea that I had entertained but had finally decided against. I will never forget what he said to me, while he was on the verge of tears: "You could open up the Orthodox branch of the International

Mission Board!" We were touched and flattered by his persistent attempts to keep us around, but we knew that this idea would simply not work.

We assured him that we were as sorry to leave as he was to see us go. He finally gave up, and made one request of us: that we not tell anyone why we were leaving until after we had arrived home. He wanted first to protect us from incessant questions and possible scorn from colleagues and Baptist nationals, and second to make sure that our organization's mission was not undermined. We had no desire to do anything that could possibly hurt our employer, so we wholeheartedly agreed.

We asked Ted if we could have six weeks to sell most of our things, pack the rest, and say goodbye to all our friends. He readily agreed, and wished us the best. Even though he could not understand why we wanted to do what we were planning to do, he was still kind and supportive of us as people.

After having talked with Ted and Teresa for over two hours, we drove back to Banja Luka, relieved that this difficult step was over with. Now we were faced with the difficult task of preparing for another cataclysmic change in our lives. Once again, we would be starting over.

Final Departure

For the eleventh time in as many years of marriage, Jennifer and I began the process of packing all our things and moving. This time, however, we had more possessions than ever before, because for the first time in our married life, Jennifer and I had planned to stay in one place for a long time. We had established our own home from scratch with our own furniture and other belongings. Now we had to get rid of them all. The new couple who had just come to the field blessed us by buying nearly all of our furniture, along with many of our other possessions. They needed furniture, and we needed to get rid of quite a bit, so the deal worked out well for all.

After we worked out all the details of our flight home, we were faced with the awkward task of telling our national and missionary friends that we were leaving, but without explaining why. We revealed the news about our resignation gradually, so as to minimize the amount of awkward time in between the announcement and our departure.

When American missionary families resign their positions and return home, it is usually due to one of a handful of reasons, including failure to adjust to the new culture, children going to college, health problems, financial problems, illegal or immoral behavior, or (too often) marriage problems. Everyone knew that our reason for leaving had nothing to do with the first two of these, and we took pains to assure everyone that it was not due to the latter four. Still, it must have sounded fishy when we repeatedly said: "We're leaving, but we can't say why. Really, though, everything is fine. Just trust us!" I don't know what everyone must have thought, but I was certain that no one guessed that we were leaving because we wanted to convert to Orthodoxy. Later, after we arrived home and told the whole story, my suspicion was confirmed. No one's theory had even been close to the truth!

Even worse than the awkwardness of not being able to tell people why we were leaving was the deep sadness we felt about leaving the country and people whom we had grown to love. Ironically, adopting their traditional faith resulted in us having to leave them. After a year and a half on the field, we had finally "arrived," both literally and figuratively. And now, we were having to give it all up. Still, we trusted that God would give us even more in return, and He certainly has.

I also realized that I needed to find a new career, at least for a while. I knew that the only field I could get into relatively easily, without the hassle and expense of years of further schooling, was teaching. Although I had taught for three years in a private school, I knew that the only way that I would be able to support our family would be to enter the public school system. Since I was not state-certified to teach, I would have to find a way to get certified. I looked into several school districts in Texas that had alternative teacher certification programs. Unfortunately, the application date for someone wanting to start teaching in the fall of 2001 had passed in all but one district. Ironically, it was the same suburban Houston district where I had attended from grades 2-12! Via e-mail, I set up an interview with the director of the alternative certification program. The interview would take place only a few days after we arrived home.

On April 21, 2001, we said goodbye one last time to our colleagues and our closest Bosnian friends. With tears in our eyes, Jennifer, Audrey, Courtney, and I left Banja Luka for the last time and drove to Zagreb. We spent the night in Zagreb at our missionary guest house, and boarded our plane the next morning. Our colleagues, and indeed our whole mission organization, treated us very well. Even though they hated to see us go, and they certainly disagreed with our new theological position, they dealt with us with the utmost of integrity and Christian love. To this day, I will not allow anyone to speak badly of Southern Baptists, particularly not missionaries, in my presence. Even though I now disagree with much of their theology and practice, I still believe that the overwhelming majority of them are kind people who love God and are seeking to serve him as best they know how. And without the Baptist church, I might never have come to have a real love for the Lord and the Scriptures. I might never have become a missionary and in so doing, discover the Orthodox Church. Both Jennifer's and my time in the Baptist church seems truly to have been used by God as a time of preparation for my entering the One, Holy, Catholic, and Apostolic Church.

Our plane touched down in Dallas later the same day that we had departed Zagreb. We were greeted at the airport by Jennifer's parents and sister, who drove us to their home in Texarkana. We were thankful to be safely back in the U. S. Now we had but a simple task ahead of us – starting our lives over from scratch!

Chapter Fourteen: An End and A Beginning

'For I know the plans I have for you,' declares the LORD, 'plans to prosper you and not to harm you, plans to give you hope and a future.'
—JEREMIAH 29:11 (NIV)

Changes

Jennifer's father, a Baptist pastor for twenty years, was not terribly excited about our decision to convert to Orthodoxy. Nevertheless, he and the rest of Jennifer's family were very glad to have us home for good. Our first few days at their house were a wonderful time of rest, relaxation, and getting caught up. Still, I had to start working on getting a job – and fast. On the evening of Audrey's tenth birthday, I boarded a Greyhound bus bound for Houston and headed to my parents' house just north of the city. My mission was threefold: buy a car (we hadn't owned one for nearly five years), get accepted into the alternative teacher certification program in my former school district, and get a teaching job in the district. I stayed at my parents' house for about a week, and in that time I succeeded in the first two parts of my mission. Unfortunately, however, I did not land a firm job offer, although I did have several leads.

While in Houston, I decided to visit an Antiochian Orthodox parish that I had found on the internet – St. Joseph's, in the west part of town. Their website was excellent, and their parish priest looked even more impressive. Father Matthew MacKay had a long beard, just like one would expect an Orthodox priest to have, and he looked resplendent in his vestments. It took me nearly an hour to get to St. Joseph's from my parents' house, but it was well worth the drive! The music was beautiful, the Liturgy itself majestic, and the people friendly. After the service, when the people went up to venerate the Cross, I followed. Fr. Matthew greeted me warmly and asked my name and what I do for a living. A little embarrassed, I said "Well, I am a Baptist missionary...or at least I *used* to be! I just came home four days ago. I have come home in order to convert to Orthodoxy." He seemed both surprised and impressed, and he invited me to come again. Little did I know that this godly man would become my spiritual father, counselor, and dear friend. Even less did I imagine that I would eventually serve this parish as a deacon and then become its assistant priest.

A few days later, I returned to Texarkana to rejoin my family. By this time, Jennifer was nearly eight months pregnant, and so naturally, I did not want to be away from her if I could help it. By the first Sunday that we were all in Texarkana, Jennifer and I were eager to attend a Divine Liturgy together. Unfortunately, there is no Orthodox parish close to Texarkana (God grant that this will change soon!). So, on the first Sunday in May, we loaded the kids into the car and drove an hour and forty-five minutes to St. Nicholas Antiochian Orthodox Church in Shreveport, Louisiana. We loved the service, and the people were as friendly as those at St. Joseph's had been. Their priest at the time, Fr. John Morris, was very kind and patient, staying after the Liturgy for more than half an hour to answer the many questions that we had. We liked it so much that we returned again the next Sunday.

A week or so after our second visit to St. Nicholas' I received a phone call that changed my life. My uncle had called to inform me that my mother had suffered a massive stroke, but that she was stable. By now, it was near the end of May, and I was reluctant to leave my great-with-child wife. My uncle said that he did not think it was imperative that I immediately come to Houston. Mom's life was not in danger, and she seemed to be improving. A couple of days later, however, my brother Cleland called to say that Mom did not seem to be improving any more. She was paralyzed on her left side, and she could not speak intelligibly. After hearing that, I immediately left to go and be with her. Sadly, my brother's description of her condition was right on target. I wept over the sight of my mother. She had always been active and full of life, and she had always loved to talk. Now she could neither walk nor talk. To make things worse, my father had been suffering from Alzheimer's disease for over five years, and Mom had been his primary caretaker. Who would take care of him now? My uncle agreed to take him in temporarily, and this relieved our stress for a while. But my brother and sisters and I were now faced with some very hard decisions.

After about a week with my parents, I returned to be with Jennifer again. I was scheduled to start my classes for the alternative certification program on June 4, which was three days past Jennifer's due date. Needless to say, we were all on pins and needles. Our mission board, on our kind former boss Ted's urging, had granted us two extra months of medical insurance, and we also had a couple of months of severance pay. Still, I had no job. Jennifer and I agreed that she and the kids would stay with her parents in Texarkana during the summer. I would spend the weekdays in Houston job-hunting and attending classes required for certification and go back to Texarkana on the weekends to be with the family. Finally, on June 9, our third daughter, Elizabeth, was born. We were overjoyed, but our joy was mixed with the sorrow of my parents' situation, and also with my having to be away from Jennifer and the kids so much.

During the summer of 2001, when I was not working on my teacher certification or spending time with my family, I began working on another project: the conversion of my friends and colleagues to Orthodoxy! I was on fire for the Ancient Faith, and I could not wait to persuade all my friends, both missionaries and non-missionaries, to become Orthodox. The need to become Orthodox had been so obvious to Jennifer and me. I assumed that if my friends read the same books that we had, and if I just explained to them my reasons for converting, they could not help but convert also!

This thinking turned out to be very naïve. While some of our missionary friends thought we had lost our mind, reacting with anger and sadness to the news of our conversion to Orthodoxy, most of our closest friends that I spoke to respected our decision. A few of them agreed with some of the thinking that had led us to the decision, but even these were not very interested in making such a big jump themselves. They were simply too committed to evangelical distinctives and too put off by some Orthodox beliefs and practices. When I loaned them my copies of *Becoming Orthodox* and my other reading materials, they politely accepted them. But if they read them, they were not persuaded as we had been. After I loaned *The Way* to one close friend, the husband in the couple who had moved from Russia to Banja Luka while we had been in Tuzla, he gave it back a few days later saying, "I'm not going to read this! The author called me a heretic in the first chapter!"

For the next couple of years, I would continue conversing with friends about Orthodoxy, but to my great disappointment, nothing I said led anyone we knew to become Orthodox. Even more sadly, our new beliefs caused a strain in nearly all of our friendships and even ended some. As a result, we found ourselves having to start over in more ways than one.

Soon after our daughter Beth was born, I was hired to teach seventh and eighth grade math. Although I had really wanted to teach high school, I was just thankful to have a job. A few weeks later, I found us an apartment in Houston near the school. We all moved to the apartment in July, and I started teaching the next month. Now, I was facing one of the greatest challenges of my life: persuading a bunch of hormone-driven seventh and eighth graders to want to learn math! Jennifer and I had frozen in Prague, battled drought and angry nationals in Tuzla, been evacuated from Banja Luka, had nearly been snowed under in Sarajevo, and had experienced a crisis of faith that led to the end of our careers. After all this, I thought that teaching in the good old U.S.A. would be easy. Boy was I wrong!

Sorrow and Joy

Our first year back in the states was filled with many sorrows. First of all, we suffered from reverse culture shock, greatly missing the job, the city, and the people that we loved.

Often we longed to go back to our former lives, but of course that was impossible for many reasons.

Also, teaching junior high school math turned out to be one of the hardest things I had ever attempted. My only previous teaching experience had been at a non-denominational Christian school, where all the kids came from stable, devout Christian families. They were not all greatly motivated, but all were at least well-behaved. But in the public school where I now taught, many of my students would regularly say and do things that neither I nor my students at the Christian school would have even dreamed of. I found the amount of disrespect that I received on a daily basis to be simply unbelievable, and the majority of my students had no semblance of a work ethic whatsoever. Things gradually improved over the course of the school year as I built relationships with my students, and some students even actually seemed to like me by the end of the first semester. Still, this did not stop me from applying for a transfer to high school in January.

Another sorrow we experienced involved our second daughter Courtney. While still in Banja Luka, we noticed that Courtney had been slow to start talking. We assumed that she was merely confused because she was hearing two languages on a regular basis, and that soon after we were in the U.S., her speaking ability would blossom. This did not happen, however, and so we had her evaluated for possible developmental problems. We were devastated when we received the news that our beautiful, beloved little girl had autism. We soon had her enrolled in a special program for children with autism in our school district, and we also obtained other types of help for her. Although she has learned much and developed somewhat, raising her has been a great challenge, filled with frustration but also with occasional joy. As of this writing, Courtney, at age nine, still cannot talk beyond a few simple words. Although we have prayed for her healing, and that she might live a "normal" life, Jennifer and I have also learned much from Courtney. Perhaps the greatest lesson of all has been to love and accept

Courtney for who she is – a beautiful gift from God – and not for what we want her to be.

Meanwhile, my parents' health continued to decline. After my mother was released from the hospital, Cleland, Lisa, and I had to put both her and my father into an assisted living facility. Fortunately, we found a place near where my brother and sister were living at the time. This facility had a regular assisted living section, where my mother would live, and a separate wing for Alzheimer's patients. This made visiting my parents much easier, since they were under the same roof. Also, they were able to have most of their meals together. Still, my mother was severely depressed, and I could tell that her will to live was ebbing away.

One day near the end of the 2001-2002 school year, while I was proctoring the state exam, there was a knock on my classroom door. One of our office staff opened the door and told me, "Mr. Early, there's a phone call for you. You really need to answer it in the office." It was my brother Cleland. He told me that my mother had died. I was shocked and did not know what to do or say. I told the office worker what had happened, and she agreed to arrange for my class to be covered. I ran to my car and drove straight to the hospital where she had died. She had suffered a heart attack. I was devastated. Even though she had lived a good, long life of eighty years, I still had so many things that I wanted to do with her and tell her. The following Sunday was to be our Chrismation, and she had been planning to attend it. Although she was not Orthodox, she had grown to love the Lord in her later years, and she had even expressed a good deal of interest in Orthodoxy. I believe that she is now with the Lord Jesus, awaiting me. To this day, I miss her greatly.

Despite all the sorrow we experienced, our first year back from Bosnia contained some joyful experiences. First of all, I had the privilege of meeting Fr. Peter Gillquist, the man whose book had started us on our journey to Orthodoxy, and hearing him speak. We first heard him speak at an Advent retreat in Houston in December. Immediately after he finished, I walked up to him and said, "I would like to thank you for ruining my career!" Of course, he was puzzled, and politely asked, "Ruined your career? What do you mean?" I told him our story and how grateful I was that he had written *Becoming Orthodox*. I wanted him to know that fifteen years after the book first appeared, God is still using it to bring people into his Church.

Another blessing I experienced was having the privilege of meeting Fr. Gordon Walker and spending a few days with him and his wife Mary Sue in their beautiful, peaceful home near Franklin, Tennessee. As he had earlier via e-mail, Fr. Gordon patiently answered the many questions that I had about Orthodoxy, the priesthood, and many other topics. I attended as many services as I could at St. Ignatius' Orthodox Church, which Fr. Gordon had founded many years before, and was greatly blessed by all. The area around Franklin was so beautiful, peaceful and quiet, that I thought about calling Jennifer and telling her to pack up the kids and our stuff and come join me! The time I spent in Franklin with Fr. Gordon and the community of St. Ignatius, though brief, was like attending a spiritual retreat.

Finally, the 2001-2002 school year ended with one of the most joyful experiences of our lives: our Chrismation, our children's baptism, and our first Holy Communion. We were now finally full-fledged Orthodox Christians! The process that had begun a year and half ago was at last complete. Now I was ready to immerse myself in the life of the parish and to begin my preparations for my new calling to the Holy Priesthood.

The End of the Beginning

In the fall of 2002, I began my studies in the St. Stephen's Course of Orthodox Theological Studies. St. Stephen's is a predominantly correspondence course designed for anyone interested in deepening their knowledge of Orthodoxy. In the Antiochian Archdiocese, it is the minimum educational requirement for someone interested in being ordained as a deacon. In addition, with his bishop's approval, a man who has converted to Orthodoxy from another Christian tradition and who has a Master of Divinity degree from a non-Orthodox seminary can substitute the St. Stephen's course for a degree from an Orthodox seminary, and can thus be considered for ordination to the Holy Priesthood.

Since I did have a Master of Divinity from a Southern Baptist seminary, Fr. Matthew encouraged me to ask my bishop's (Bishop BASIL) blessing to enroll in St. Stephen's. Bishop BASIL agreed, and I jumped into my studies with gusto. Each semester, I was sent a list of books to read and a set of study questions to guide my reading. At the end of the semester, I then had to write between seven and ten essays on the readings. The best part of the program, however, was the three weeks, one week per year, that I was required to spend at the Antiochian Village in Ligionier, Pennsylvania.

At the Antiochian village, I had the chance to listen to lectures given by our professors and other gifted teachers, and to fellowship with other students from around the country (and, increasingly, the world). We worshipped at least twice a day, and to make things even better, the food was great! Though often physically exhausting, these three weeks were spiritually fulfilling, and I will always cherish them.

During the time I was studying for ordination, my work situation also improved. In June of 2002, I was hired to teach Algebra I and Geometry at a high school near our home. I was now able to work with older and more mature students and to teach more challenging coursework. The next year, I was given the privilege of teaching Advanced Placement Statistics, a brand new course for our campus. I rounded out my teaching schedule with Geometry, which had students who were older and generally more mature than Algebra students. Our living situation also improved when we bought our first house. We now had plenty of room for our girls, and as an added bonus, I was only about a mile from the high school where I taught. I was blessed to be able to pick up extra work assignments so that Jennifer could stay home with Beth.

In the years after our Chrismation, Jennifer and I continued to grow in our practice and appreciation of the Orthodox faith. Shortly after we were received into the

Church, I began serving as a chanter at St. Joseph's. Later, I began teaching adult Sunday School, served as an altar server, and sang in the choir. By the end of 2003, Fr. Matthew suggested that it was time for me to apply for ordination to the Holy Diaconate. I was humbled and yet excited at this great opportunity.

During this time of spiritual growth, my father's health continued to deteriorate. In April of 2003, he suffered a massive stroke, which his doctor said would be fatal. Still, like the tough old Marine that he was, he recovered, although he could no longer swallow and had to be fed through a feeding tube. In June of the next year, I received a phone call from my brother-in-law Jace, who said simply, "We lost the Colonel." Even though I had been able to grieve for several years while my father gradually succumbed to the ravages of Alzheimer's disease, I was still devastated when he finally passed on. No mortal man had been more influential in my life, nor will any ever be. My father served his country in uniform for twenty-six years, and he trained young men and women to do so for another twelve. He taught me right from wrong, along with the great value of clean living and of excelling in all that I do. May God have mercy upon his soul.

Soon, our sorrow turned to joy again. On the very same day as my father's passing, Jennifer and I received an unanticipated blessing. Once again, we were expecting a child! Nine months later, in January of 2005, we welcomed our fourth daughter, Christine Grace, into the world. Christine is a beautiful and sweet child. She helps keep Jennifer and me young!

Meanwhile, in August of 2004, I was blessed to be ordained to the Holy Diaconate by Bishop BASIL. Serving as a deacon under the godly tutelage of Fr. Matthew was a wonderful experience. Fr. Matthew was also grateful for the help around the altar, for he had been serving alone for ten years. I, in turn, was grateful to be able to help him!

The following November, when Bishop BASIL was visiting our parish, he gave me his blessing to apply for ordination to the Holy Priesthood. My application was accepted by the Archdiocese, and with joy that I cannot describe, on February 12, 2006, the goal that I had been working toward for over five years was at last fulfilled. Finally, I was an Orthodox priest!

Since then, it has been my pleasure to serve with Fr. Matthew at St. Joseph. In one sense, I feel like this time I really have finally "arrived." But I know that in reality, this is just the beginning. I am certain that God has even more planned for Jennifer and me in the future. Until then, I plan to serve the Lord with fear and trembling, but also with joy. My life up to this point has been a wild ride, but I wouldn't trade it for anything. To God be the glory forever! Amen!

Appendix:

How to Turn an Evangelical Protestant into an Orthodox Christian in Four Easy Steps

Of course, the subtitle of this section is written totally tongue-in-cheek. I realize that no one will convert to the Orthodox faith unless the Holy Spirit first draws him or her. Still, I am often asked, "What would be a good book to give to my friend /co-worker /son /daughter /parent /cousin (etc.) who is asking me about Orthodoxy?" On other occasions, I have been asked, "I have read such and such book; what should I read next?"

Of course, many other priests', writers,' and thinkers' recommendations would be somewhat (or perhaps totally) different from mine. Still, I thought that the reader might be interested in knowing the books that I personally recommend to evangelical inquirers, and the order in which I recommend that they read them. For more information on the books, see the bibliography.

Step One: *Becoming Orthodox*, by Fr. Peter Gillquist
Step Two: *Thirsting for God*, by Matthew Gallatin
Step Three: *The Way*, by Clark Carlton
Step Four: *Common Ground*, by Fr. Jordan Bajis

In addition to the above steps, I would urge an inquirer to read through the *Orthodox Study Bible*, New Testament, carefully reading the study notes and the explanatory articles that are sprinkled throughout the text.

For those who do not much care for reading, I recommend *An Eastern Orthodox Response to Evangelical Claims* by Fr. Paul O'Callaghan and the series of topical pamphlets published by Conciliar Press, especially the titles that I recommend in my "Other Recommended Resources" section.

What about Roman Catholics?

For Roman Catholic inquirers, I recommend the following books:

Step One: *Orthodoxy and Catholicism: What Are the Differences?* by Fr. Ted Pulcini

Step Two: *Popes and Patriarchs* by Michael Whelton

Step Three: *The Truth* by Clark Carlton

Step Four: *Common Ground*

Annotated Bibliography

Bajis, Fr. Jordan, *Common Ground: An Introduction to Orthodox Christianity for the American Christian.* Minneapolis: Light and Life Publishing, 1991. This is a scholarly, well-researched, and persuasive book. It was particularly helpful in winning me over to the Orthodox position on infant baptism and on the authoritative nature of Holy Tradition, but it also has excellent chapters on salvation and Sola Scriptura.

Carlton, Clark, *The Way: What Every Protestant Should Know About the Orthodox Church.* Salisbury, MA: Regina Orthodox Press, 1997. As I mentioned in the text, reading this book put the nail in the coffin of my being an evangelical. This is a very persuasive book, particularly regarding *Sola Scriptura* vs. Tradition and the structure and style of Orthodox worship. One caveat: this book is not for the thin-skinned! It should probably not be the first book that an evangelical reads about Orthodoxy, unless he or she is already on the path to conversion.

Gillquist, Fr. Peter, *Becoming Orthodox: A Journey to the Ancient Christian Faith,* revised edition. Ben Lomond, CA: Conciliar Press, 1992. This is the book that started me on my pilgrimage to Orthodoxy. It is very well-written and inspiring story that reads like a novel in places. This is the first book that I give to evangelical friends who are curious about Orthodoxy. It is persuasive yet irenic in tone, and it is simply a great and inspiring story.

The Orthodox Study Bible: New Testament and Psalms, New King James Version. Nashville: Thomas Nelson, 1993. An essential read for all Orthodox Christians and for all non-Orthodox Christians who desire to understand the Orthodox understanding of Scripture.

Roberts, Alexander, and James Donaldson, *The Ante Nicene Fathers, Volume 1: The Apostolic Fathers, Justin Martyr, Irenaeus,* **fourth printing. Peabody, MA: Hendrikson, 2004.** This is part of the magisterial series that includes English translations of the Pre-Nicene, Nicene, and Post-Nicene Fathers. Translated by leading Anglican scholars of the nineteenth century, the translation is generally reliable, even if the notes are often not.

Sparks, Fr. Jack, ed., *The Apostolic Fathers.* **Minneapolis: Light and Life Publishing, 1978.** A more recent and readable translation than *The Ante-Nicene Fathers,* translated by twentieth-century non-Orthodox scholars, with introductions and notes by Sparks, an Orthodox priest who converted to Orthodoxy in the late 1970's.

Ware, Timothy (Bishop Kallistos), *The Orthodox Church,* **fourth edition. London: Penguin Books, 1997.** Perhaps the most widely read and best-selling English language book on Orthodoxy, this book is generally recognized as the standard introduction to the Orthodox faith. Unlike the works by Bajis, Carlton, and Gillquist, this work does not seek to persuade the reader of the superiority of Orthodoxy to other Christian traditions, but simply presents a solid and highly readable overview of Orthodox history and doctrine.

Other Recommended Resources

Carlton, Clark, *The Faith*. Salisbury, MA: Regina Orthodox Press, 1997. Used in catechumen classes in Orthodox parishes around the country, this book is an outstanding, easy to read overview of the Orthodox faith.

Carlton, Clark, *The Life*. Salisbury, MA: Regina Orthodox Press, 1997. A must read for all evangelical Protestants, especially those who struggle with the Orthodox theology of salvation. In this book, Carlton argues persuasively against *Sola Fide* and "once saved always saved," among other things.

Carlton, Clark, *The Truth*. Salisbury, MA: Regina Orthodox Press, 1999. This is the equivalent of *The Way* for Roman Catholics. Protestants would do well to read it too, particularly Chapter Three, which is the best argument against the "Satisfaction" theory of atonement taken granted by most Protestants as well as Roman Catholics

Coniaris, Fr. Anthony, *Introducing the Orthodox Church*. Mineapolis: Light and Life Publishing, 1982. Just what it says—an outstanding overview of all aspects of Orthodoxy, covering more topics that *The Orthodox Church*, but going into less detail.

Elder Cleopa of Romania, *The Truth of Our Faith*. Ben Lomond, CA: Conciliar Press, 2000. Written by the saintly abbot (now with the Lord) of a monastery in Romania, this book is similar to Fr. O'Callaghan's pamphlet (see below), but less broad and more deep. This would be especially helpful for evangelicals from a Reformed or Calvinistic background.

Gallatin, Matthew, *Thirsting for God in a Land of Shallow Wells*. Ben Lomond, CA: Conciliar Press, 2002. This book was not published until after my family and I were Chrismated, but we still found it helpful in confirming the truth of our new faith. I simply cannot recommend this book highly enough to evangelical inquirers. It is a kinder, gentler version of *The Way* that covers more topics, albeit in less depth than Carlton's books.

Gillquist, Fr. Peter, ed. *Coming Home: Why Protestant Clergy are Becoming Orthodox.* Ben Lomond, CA: Conciliar Press, 1992. A series of gripping stories about how a wide variety of Protestant ministers, from high church Anglican to "holy roller" Pentecostal, found their way to Orthodoxy.

Mathewes-Green, Frederica, *At the Corner of East and Now: A Modern Life in Ancient Christian Orthodoxy.* New York: Tarcher/Putnam, 1999. Mathewes-Green, a prolific writer, popular speaker and wife of an Orthodox priest, combines vignettes about life in her parish, Orthodoxy in general, and living the life of an Orthodox Christian in the world.

Nieuwsma, Virginia, ed. *Our Heart's True Home.* Ben Lomond, CA: Conciliar Press, 1996. Similar to *Coming Home*, but written by and primarily for women.

O'Callaghan, Fr. Paul. *An Eastern Orthodox Response to Evangelical Claims.* Minneapolis: Light and Life Publishing, 1984. Fr. Paul lists several common questions that evangelicals ask about Orthodoxy and answers them briefly but persuasively.

Pulcini, Fr. Theodore, *Orthodoxy and Catholicism: What are the Differences?* Ben Lomond, CA: Conciliar Press, 1995. This is my favorite work on Orthodoxy *vis-à-vis* Roman Catholicism, written in a completely irenic tone by a former Roman Catholic who is now an Orthodox priest and scholar. This would be a great resource to give to a Roman Catholic friend, and it has the added bonus of being very brief (25 pages).

Whelton, Thomas, *Popes and Patriarchs: An Orthodox Perspective on Roman Catholic Claims*. Ben Lomond, CA: Conciliar Press, 2006. This is a well-reasoned, recently published discussion of the issues that separate Orthodox Christians and Roman Catholics. Whelton also wrote a similar but more extensive book entitled *Two Paths* (Regina Orthodox Press) in 1998.

Whiteford, Fr. John, *Sola Scriptura: An Orthodox Analysis of the Cornerstone of Reformation Theology*. Ben Lomond, CA: Conciliar Press, 1996. This is the most thorough treatment of the many problems with *Sola Scriptura* that I have ever read. I wish all evangelical Protestants would read it!

In addition to these books, Conciliar Press publishes a set of short (15-30 page) pamphlets on various beliefs and practices of the Orthodox Church that differ from those of Protestants. The ones that I found the most instrumental in convincing me of the truth of Orthodoxy include *Finding the New Testament Church,* by Fr. Jon Braun, *Scripture and Tradition*, by Raymond (Fr. Thomas) Zell, *Which Came First, the Church or the New Testament?*, by Fr. James Bernstein, *How to Read Your Bible,* by Bishop Kallistos Ware, *Entering God's Kingdom* and *Finishing the Race* (both on the Orthodox concept of salvation), by Fr. Peter Gillquist, and *Heavenly Worship*, by Fr. Richard Ballew. Also, Conciliar Press has just published a pamphlet called *Infant Baptism*, by Fr. John Hainsworth, which would be especially helpful for Baptists and other evangelicals that believe that only adults and older children should be baptized. Conciliar offers a total of 31 of these pamphlets, and all of them are excellent. Visit www.conciliarpress.com for more information.

There are two other Orthodox publishers that specialize in communicating the truth and beauty of Orthodoxy to the non-Orthodox world. Both of these publishers offer a multitude of resources that space does not permit me to list here. I encourage you to visit their websites for more information. The two publishers are Light and Life Publishers (www.light-n-life.com) and Regina Orthodox Press (www.reginaorthodoxpress.com).

0800 - 093 - 93 - 94